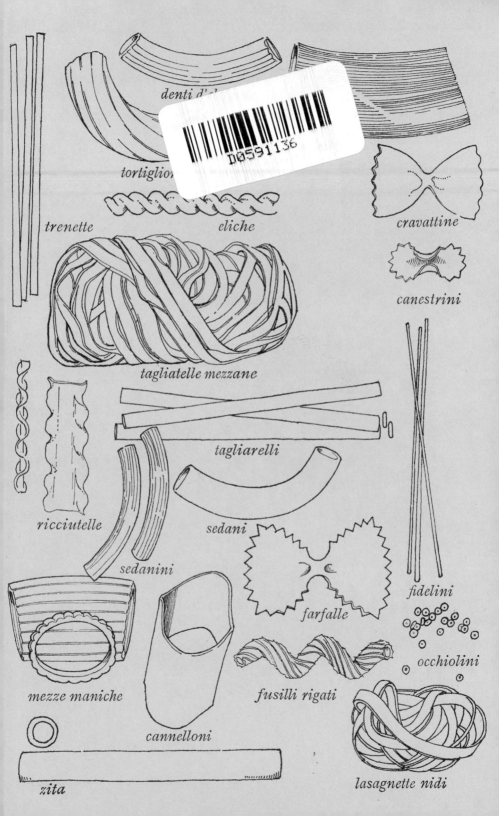

denti d'...

tortiglion...

trenette

eliche

cravattine

canestrini

tagliatelle mezzane

ricciutelle

tagliarelli

sedani

sedanini

farfalle

fidelini

occhiolini

mezze maniche

cannelloni

fusilli rigati

zita

lasagnette nidi

THE PASTA COOK BOOK

By the same author

Balkan Cooking
A Cook's Tour
Cooking from the Commonwealth
A Dictionary of Gastronomy
  (with André L. Simon)
Far Eastern Cookery
French Cooking
German Cooking
Greek Cooking
Italian Cooking
Regional Italian Cookery
Making your own Preserves
Poultry and Game

Rice Cooking
Russian Cooking
Soups
Sultan's Pleasure (with Pauline Espir)
Traditional Home Cooking
Common Market Cheeses
Common Market Dishes
Common Market Wines

In preparation:

Central European Cooking
Eating in India
Eating in France

THE
PASTA COOK BOOK

Robin Howe

BOOK CLUB EDITION

This edition published by
Purnell Book Services Limited
St. Giles House, 49/50 Poland Street, WIA 2LG
by arrangement with André Deutsch Limited

Printed in Great Britain by
Ebenezer Baylis & Son Limited
The Trinity Press, Worcester, and London

CONTENTS

Acknowledgements   *page* 7

Notes on Comparative Cookery Terms and Measures   8

Chart of Cooking Times for Boiling Pasta in Water   10

Chart of Cooking Times for Boiling Pasta in Stock   12

Introduction — The World of Pasta   13

1 General Instructions for Cooking Pasta   23

2 Soups   37

3 Fish   44

4 Savoury Top-of-the-Stove   54

   (i)   MACARONI   54

   (ii) NOODLES   63

   (iii) SPAGHETTI   72

   (iv) SMALL SHAPES   87

5 Baked   91

6 Left-Overs   118

7 Salads   124

8 Sauces, Dressings, Stuffings   128

9 Sweet Dishes   141

10 Children's Dishes   151

   Index   155

LIST OF PLATES

Between pages 32–33

1 Sweet Macaroni Pudding
2 Spaghetti with Tunny Fish

Between pages 64–65

3 Baked Macaroni and Canned Salmon Custard
(before and after baking)
4 Macaroni with Black Olives and Salami
5 'Straw and Hay' or Noodles with a Cream Sauce
6 Noodles with Pesto

Between pages 96–97

7 Noodles with Brandy Raisin Sauce
8a Noodles with a Piquant Sauce
8b Spaghetti with an Uncooked Tomato Sauce
9a Macaroni with a Pine Nut Sauce
9b Stuffed Macaroni Shepherdess Style
10a Macaroni with Broccoli
10b Spaghetti and Sweet Pepper Salad

Between pages 128–129

11 Macaroni au Gratin
12 Empress Soufflé

TO
VINCENZO AGNESI
WHO TAUGHT ME TO APPRECIATE
PASTA

ACKNOWLEDGEMENTS

It was once the fashion for an author to dedicate a book to her or his husband or wife 'without whom this book would never have been written'. Sometimes this was probably true. It is, however, quite certain that without the help of Eva Agnesi this book on pasta would never have seen the light of day. Nor, indeed, without the aid of my husband who not only helped me to write it but also helped me to cook and eat my way through over two hundred dishes prepared from the recipes in this book.

COMPARATIVE COOKERY TERMS AND MEASURES

Throughout this book both British and American measurements have been used and, wherever possible, ingredients have been measured in cups and tablespoons for easy conversion. The British measurement has been printed first, followed by the American equivalent in brackets.

The British measuring cup used is the British Standard Institute's cup which gives a $\frac{1}{2}$-pint measure, the equivalent to 10 fluid ounces, and is the size of the average British breakfast-cup or tumbler. The American standard cup is equal to the American $\frac{1}{2}$ pint, which is the equivalent of 8 fluid ounces.

All spoon measurements are level throughout this book unless otherwise stated.

CONVERSION OF METRIC MEASURES INTO BRITISH MEASURES

Exact measurements are not possible, and if applied in the kitchen would require every housewife-cook to be a mathematician. It is probably best, therefore, to aim for the nearest approximation, as below:

Exact Measurements
1 kilogram = 2·2 lb   1 litre = 1·8 pints

Approximate Measurements Used
1 lb = 0·5 kg or 500 grams   1 gallon = 4·5 litres
8 oz = 240 grams   1 quart = 1·125 litres (1$\frac{1}{8}$ litres)
4 oz = 120 grams   1 pint   = 0·5 litres
1 oz =   30 grams $\frac{1}{2}$ pint = 0·25 litres
                                 $\frac{1}{4}$ pint = 0·125 litres ($\frac{1}{8}$ litre)

OVEN TEMPERATURE CHART

Oven Description	Electric Oven Setting, Approximate Temperature	Gas Thermostat
very cool	250°F. (130°C.)	$\frac{1}{4}$
very cool	275°F. (140°C.)	$\frac{1}{2}$
cool	300°F. (150°C.)	1, 2
warm	325°F. (160°C.)	3
moderate	350°F. (180°C.)	4
fairly hot	375°F. (190°C.)	5
fairly hot	400°F. (200°C.)	6
hot	425°F. (220°C.)	7
very hot	450°F. (230°C.)	8
very hot	475°F. (240°C.)	9

Note: unless otherwise stated the servings for the recipes in this book are for 4–6 people.

COOKING TIME FOR BOILING PASTA IN WATER

Generally pasta manufacturers print the correct cooking timings for their products on their packets. However, from time to time one comes across economy packages without timings. The following timetable applies to all of the pasta shapes mentioned in this book, also to similar shapes. It must be noted that pasta cooked in stock takes longer than when cooked in water.

Shape	Minutes
Abissini	15
Bucatini	7
Capelli d'angelo (very fine vermicelli)	1–2
Chifferotti	8
Chifferotti rigati	12
Cravattine	10
Denti d'elefante	12
Eliche	8
Farfalle	12
Fettuccine and Fettuccine nidi	6
Fidelini	5
Fusilli	6
Fusilli rigati	8
Gnocchi	11
Lasagne	15
Lasagnette and Lasagnette nidi	5
Linguine	6
Lumaconi	11
Maccheroni	9
Maccheroni rigati	9
Maniche and Mezze Maniche	11

Millerighe	8
Nidi di reginette	7
Penne	6
Ricciutelle	8
Spaghetti	10
Spaghettini	8
Tagliarelli	9
Tagliatelle	8
Tagliatelle mezzane	9
Tortiglioni	18
Trenette	9
Zita	9

COOKING TIME FOR BOILING
PASTA IN STOCK

Anellini	12
Avemaria	14
Capelli d'angelo (very fine vermicelli)	1–2
Capellini	2
Chifferini rigati	13
Chinesini	13
Ditalini	12
Occhi di pernice	9
Pennini piccoli	12
Pisellini	15
Puntette	18
Stellette	19

THE WORLD OF PASTA

What a wonderful world it is, that warm and cheerful world where pasta is eaten every day. Boccaccio describes its careless abundance in the *Decameron*, 'And there was a whole mountain of grated Parmesan cheese, upon which people did nothing else but make macaroni and ravioli and cook them in chicken broth: then they threw them down the hillside and the more the people caught, the more they had.'

Pasta has its literature – mainly Italian. Casanova, of all people, wrote an ode to spaghetti while Rossini composed the overture to *Othello* on a diet of macaroni and is said to have loved his food as he loved life and music. It is told of him too that, being accosted by someone who reminded him they had met at a dinner, he replied: 'I remember the macaroni but not your face.'

In 1949 Giuseppe Marotta, a Neapolitan, wrote: 'He who enters paradise through a door is not a Neapolitan. We make our entrance into that heavenly abode by parting a curtain of spaghetti. As soon as we are weaned from our mother's breast we are fed a fragment of spaghetti ... What better inheritance can I leave my sons than spaghetti.'

And, indeed, this is just what a Genoese soldier did do in 1279. He left his heirs a basket of macaroni. The authenticated will, now in the state archives, is a document which satisfies the Italian ego, for it proves beyond doubt that the secret of pasta-making was not brought back from China by Marco Polo and his sailors as is so often alleged.* This document is described in the archives as 'the most ancient and authenticated news about macaroni'. It is a deed made out by the notary Ugolino Scarpa on 4 February,

---

* Marco Polo, it must be remembered, did not return to Italy from his Far Eastern travels until 1292.

1279, and it gives a list of what the soldier, Ponzio Bastone, was leaving to his heirs. It includes a *bariscella plena de macaronis*, that is, a small basket, full of macaroni. According to Professor Calvini, who is an authority on the subject, this is the first real evidence concerning macaroni and, even more important, it is evidently about dried macaroni. Probably the basket contained small *gnocchi* made by hand and dried in the sun.

But when and how was pasta invented?

We know that the first pasta was made quite simply with flour and water, but whether this dish appeared first in China or in Italy no one will ever really know. There is said to be mention of macaroni in the *Hon Zo*, a Chinese cookery book, dating from about 3000 BC, which describes more than one kind of macaroni and gives various recipes for cooking it.

However, the question of whether the Chinese had pasta before the Italians, or vice versa, is not disputed in Italy. They do not much care. What they do resent is the idea that they learned the art of pasta-making from the Chinese.

There is archaeological evidence of early pasta-making in the Etruscan Tomb of Reliefs which shows the interior of an Etruscan house of the fourth century BC not far from Civitavecchia. Among the stucco reliefs some gadgets which a housewife would have needed to make her pasta have been identified. The *spianadora*, or the board on which she worked her dough, the receptacle to contain flour, even a rolling-pin. And to remove any further doubt, there is even a cog wheel with a long handle reproduced on the same pillar on which the *spianadora* is carved. The cog wheel could only have been used to cut shapes of dough into macaroni.

Although throughout Italian literature pasta has been called by various names, macaroni, lasagne, fideli, vermicelli, etc., today, for Italians, all shapes are collectively known as pasta. But elsewhere pasta products have assumed different labels. For many foreigners spaghetti *is* pasta, the only kind they really know. Others talk collectively of noodles though this is a word of German origin, *Nudeln*. In America pasta becomes macaroni.

Macaroni is an old name but its etymology is obscure. In 1041 we find the word *mackarone* but not referring to pasta at all but to someone being stupid. It has been suggested the name came from the Greek word for grass, *macoirionon*, so named because of its long leaves, or from the diminutive of *macaira*, blade, or just as likely from *macareo*, Greek to make happy.

But in Naples they have their own explanation. They declare it was the expression of rapture uttered by a Neapolitan cardinal on being presented with a dish of macaroni for the first time. '*Ma caroni*,' he called them, which translated means 'my little dears'. An unlikely but pretty story.

Most non-Italians are inclined to think of macaroni as a short, thick, round shape, but this was and is by no means the case. In Naples we still find thick, long macaroni. Among the early references to the eating of macaroni, we have this from the fourteenth-century Italian writer, Franco Sacchetti: '. . . then hot macaroni is brought to the table . . . Having mixed and rolled it up, Noddo swallows.' It seems likely, in fact certain, that this macaroni was long. Also it is certain that Italians used a fork to eat pasta, as they do today.

The name spaghetti comes from *spago*, meaning string, which makes spaghetti 'little strings' and reminds us that, strictly speaking, we should treat spaghetti as a plural, as the Italians do.

Spaghetti in its early days was called fideli and the dialect word *fidei* is still used in parts of Liguria. Today fidelini is a long pasta, thicker than angel's hair (capelli d'angelo) but thinner than spaghetti.

Spaghetti is not an old word, although the whole world knows it, and we find that in Naples, for instance, the same shape was and is still called vermicelli. In Naples too, macaroni means only long shapes, such as zitoni, zita, maccheroncelli and bucatini.

At the turn of the present century, when pasta became more familiar in Britain, vermicelli was the word for long strands of pasta and this because the pasta-makers of Naples had the largest share of the export trade. However, over the years, the name spaghetti has superseded that of vermicelli.

It is interesting to note that in 1154 the Arab writer and geographer, Al-Idrisi, wrote a book called *Entertainment for Travellers*. In this he describes a special food 'made with flour in the shape of strings', which was manufactured at that time at Trabia near

Palermo, in Sicily. The Arabs called it *itriyah* and this word still survives in Palermo with 'vermicelli di Tria'.

Another old name for pasta was lasagne, which again was used more or less for all shapes. The writer monk, Salimbene of Parma (1221–87) writes of another monk, Giovanni of Ravenna, who had no rival in his greed for lasagne with cheese. 'I never saw a man who ate lasagne with cheese as greedily as he did.'

On 7 January, 1316, a deed was drawn up in Genoa for the renting of a house owned by Maria Borgogno who made lasagne. And two 'lasagnarii' were taken on board the galley of the *Paganino Doria*, in May 1351, to make fresh lasagne for the crew during the voyage.

Everything concerning pasta was controlled. There were laws fixing prices. For example, in Milan in 1421 it was decreed that the prices of lasagne and small macaroni should be fixed by the judges from time to time and proclaimed by public crier. Those who disobeyed were severely punished.

Also extremely important were the many guilds. A Guild of Master Fidelari was founded in Savona in 1577 while Genoa had its guilds as did 'the Most Faithful City of Naples' with its Guild of Vermicellari, founded in 1579. In Rome in 1595 and again in 1602 there were proclamations against the city's 'vermicellari' until finally they gained a hearing and formed their own guild in 1642. Often there were serious struggles, one guild against the other, and many are the edicts of those days when the City Fathers had to intervene between the quarrelling parties.

Although the Ligurians claim to have been the first to manufacture pasta, the Neapolitans soon took over from them and this despite their fondness for vegetables – especially cabbage – which had led to their being nicknamed 'the leaf-eaters'. In those days Neapolitans hardly ate any pasta and when they did it was served mainly to the rich and the sick. In fact in 1509 there was an edict forbidding the preparation of macaroni because the cost of flour had risen as a result of wars, and there were heavy punishments for those who disobeyed. In time, however, the edict was lifted and the Neapolitans became so enamoured of macaroni products that they came to be nicknamed 'the macaroni-eaters'. Probably because of the influx of Neapolitans to the United

States, all Italians became known as 'macaronis'. Damon Runyon in one of his delightful short stories had a character called The Macarone, naturally an Italian.

Macaroni was well known in Britain and was actually being imported into the country in 1772 when it was recorded that 'the word macaroni is the name of a well-known Italian dish unknown in this country before the recent peace'. It had been introduced by those rich young men who had made the Grand Tour of Europe and, because of their foppish Italiante manners, came to be dubbed 'macaronis'. These young dandies who dressed extravagantly and ate luxuriously founded their own club in Pall Mall – the Macaroni Club.

The fame, or notoriety, of the 'macaronis' spread to America where, in 1775 Edward Bangs wrote his odd little ditty which has become one of America's best known folk songs:

'Yankie Doodle came to town
Riding on a pony;
Stuck a feather in his cap
And called it macaroni.'

Whether it had anything to do with macaroni or with 'macaronis', no one is sure even though there has been much research into the origin of the song which has a revolutionary background to it.

I mentioned earlier that the Italians – who invented the fork – ate pasta with it. The Neapolitan *lazzaroni*, or street urchins, however, ate macaroni with their fingers. It seems that they did this with some skill, for Carlo Dalbone wrote in 1866: 'Using two fingers as a fork, the Neapolitan *lazzarone* raises the macaroni or vermicelli half a palm above his mouth then, slightly turning his hand, he thrusts the macaroni into his mouth with a skill which reveals a long training and without getting dirty.' In those days steaming-hot pasta dishes were sold in the streets and there were even professional macaroni eaters who excited the disgust of one Englishman, William Stamer of London, who was equally disgusted with 'Brown, Jones and Robinson' who encouraged them.

Apart from street eating, there were eating houses which served nothing but macaroni or vermicelli and they were called 'maccaronare'.

As Americans already know, they owe a great deal to that great statesman, the third President of the United States, Thomas Jefferson. He was the first man to import Lombardy poplars into America, also Tuscan wines and, later, grapevines from which he made his own wines. Among other things he tried, without much success, to introduce the Americans to pasta, which he had eaten and enjoyed when in Italy.

Jefferson made a tour of Piedmont, Lombardy and Liguria and recognized the importance of this flourishing and cheap food for his own country. Some time later he asked a friend who was travelling in Italy to get him a pasta die. The friend, William Short, did as he was requested and Jefferson dedicated himself to the task of popularizing macaroni. But his attempts were not too successful and it was not until the great influx of Italians, most of whom came from the South and were the biggest eaters of pasta, that this food took firm hold in the United States. Eventually it became universal throughout the country, albeit not always considered an elegant dish.

With all this, what then is pasta?

Briefly it is dough made from durum wheat semolina combined with water. It is pressed through dies of different shapes which can give the same dough a myriad of shapes and sizes. The finest pasta is made exclusively with this type of wheat and when you see on a packet of pasta, *pasta di semola di grano duro*, it means simply it is made with durum wheat semolina. In Italian, *semola* means flour, it also means bran, which is sometimes confusing. Good pasta should not contain bran.

There was a time when every housewife made her own pasta. Even twenty years ago this was the case. But today the Italian pasta manufacturers have brought pasta-making to such a fine art that this is no longer a common practice and I have found that it is difficult to tell a good make of factory pasta from home-made pasta or from pasta fresca, which is made in shops throughout Italy. Stuffed pastas, however, such as ravioli and tortellini are still best made either at home or bought from the many pasta shops. In time probably even they will come from a giant machine.

The War on Pasta

Surely one of the oddest 'wars' ever began in a restaurant in Rome in November, 1931. It was started by Marinetti, the philosopher and futuristic poet. His 'guns' were directed against the Italian kitchen, and his aim was to liberate the Italians from their ancient eating habits and obsessions, and in particular to wean them off pasta. Pasta, he claimed, induced laziness and brutalism, and made men gross, heavy and pessimistic.

Filippo Tommaso Marinetti certainly started a commotion. The very next day the Italian press, plus some of the pasta manufacturers and others, rose as one man in the defence of their favourite food. A mighty dispute followed producing a batch of amusing articles, jokes, cartoons and speeches, plus much serious writing. For, in the background, was Mussolini, conducting the 'Battle of the Wheat'. Although Italy was the largest producer of durum wheat a good quantity had to be imported to satisfy the home demand. To save foreign exchange Mussolini wanted to switch to ordinary wheat so as to produce more bread, and at the same time he wanted to increase rice consumption.

Marinetti, however, had his supporters and a campaign of futuristic cooking was launched. Some quite horrible concoctions were thought up and the cartoonists had a field day. One cartoon shows a chef making a *carneplastico*, or plastic stew, using half an umbrella, an old tyre and some detergent: the chef wears a gas mask as he cooks. It is served to Marinetti and the chef is presented with a medal and a laurel wreath. Another cartoon shows a woman searching for her perfume. 'Oh,' says the maid, 'don't you remember, we cooked the beans in it last night.'

The Mayor of Rome and the Duke of Bovino for the defence claimed that the angels in paradise ate nothing but vermicelli with tomatoes, to which Marinetti replied that he had always thought life among the angels must be monotonous.

Italy laughed at the antics of Marinetti and his friends who created eating conditions as bizarre as their dishes. They ate with their hands, sometimes to the accompaniment of warmed perfumes sprayed around them, so that bald-headed men (Marinetti was one) should not catch cold while they ate. Or they ate with only one hand, seeking tactile sensations by stroking a piece of

silk or velvet, or even sandpaper with the other. Perhaps also
to take their minds off what they were eating. Italians laughed
too at the futuristic compositions of red wine, lemon, cubes of
chocolate, bitter herbs and cheese, and one cartoon depicted a
chemist rubbing his hands as he tells his son their fortunes will
be made. There was another famous horror, salami in hot coffee
with 'abundant *Eau de Cologne*'.

But, although most Italians laughed, there were some who
listened. Like Goebbels' dictum about repeating an untruth often
enough, the story that pasta was fattening began to take hold. I
do not think Italians believed other extravagant claims, such as
that short legs and other physical deformities were caused by
eating pasta but, as they looked at the enticing mound of food,
served day after day with aromatic sauces, they began to have
doubts. A few, very few, refused to eat pasta. The whisper gained
strength. Today there are many who believe that it is fattening.

However, considering the gastronomic and economic advan-
tages of pasta one can see that it is not likely to be ousted from its
traditionally favoured place in the Italian cuisine. On the contrary,
with the increasing cost of food, and in particular meat, the cult
of pasta is likely to spread.

Eat Pasta and Keep Slim
'Eat pasta and keep slim' is not an empty slogan. Pasta with a
sauce and cheese is a complete food and, according to a well-
known Italian professor of human physiology at Milan Univer-
sity, it never harmed anyone. If pasta makes you fat, it is because
it is so good you may possibly eat too much of it.

But brands of pasta differ. One may retain the germ or embryo,
the living part of the wheat found inside the grain, while another
does not. We need not concern ourselves here with why the
wheat germ is sometimes omitted. What we do need to know
and remember is that from a nutritional point of view the
retention of the germ is extremely important.

Pasta prepared according to the old tradition is the best for it
still contains the germ or embryo which is a perfect food in itself
and has within it the many micro-elements necessary to the little
plant during its early development.

Over-eating has become a common habit, not just through greed but of necessity. By over-refinement the modern world has impoverished many foods and in an unconscious search for the little good left in them many people feel the need to eat more and more. This 'concealed' or 'hidden hunger', as the scientists have called it, leads to an excessive intake of food which, in turn, leads to fat.

A British doctor wrote recently: 'There is some evidence that the consumption of pasta is not only conducive to slimness but that also certain forms of heart diseases are less frequent.' He quotes the examples of Italians living in South Italy who suffer less from coronary heart diseases than Italians living in Emilia, or in Britain. The Southerners eat pasta made with semolina, which contains some of the wheat germ. The Emilians eat pasta made from flour without the germ. A French professor, member of the Higher Council of Public Health in France, gives added proof in a French medical journal.

Good pasta is made with durum wheat which contains gluten, a protein of vegetable origin. Like the white of an egg, gluten gives good cooking qualities to pasta. The best quality pasta contains as much as 14 to 15 per cent. of protein.

It is maintained that one can live on pasta exclusively as it is always accompanied by a sauce, which also contains protein. A man leading a sedentary life consumes between 2000–2500 calories a day; a woman roughly 2000. The nutritional value of one pound of pasta is about 1600 calories. One pound of pasta feeds six people and, with a sauce, does not constitute an overdose of calories.

A plate of pasta, roughly three ounces (for do not forget that good pasta grows three times its volume when cooked), when dressed with a tomato sauce and grated cheese, supplies some five hundred calories, the pasta providing three hundred and twenty of them. At the same time, it provides a significant quantity of vitamins and mineral substances in an easily assimilable form.

It is only greed that makes people fat. If more calories are consumed than the body can use, the body becomes fat by adding those excess calories to its reserve.

People ask whether pasta is easily digested. It is. It is suitable
for children, even for babies, as well as old people and invalids.

Another frequent question is: 'Is it better to eat pasta just with
butter or with a sauce?' There is no difference as far as ease of
digestion is concerned. And as to whether you should use this
or that sauce, the answer is, we should eat what we like eating,
rather on the old, old principle that 'a little of what you fancy
does you good'.

It is inevitable that any book concerned exclusively with pasta
dishes will have a strong Italian flavour. However, although by
far the largest number of pasta recipes come from Italy the
Italians are by no means the only pasta eaters for their neighbours
in Central Europe, in northern and southern Germany, Switzer-
land and France all eat large quantities of pasta and also have
evolved their own recipes. Such recipes are included in this book.

CHAPTER ONE

GENERAL INSTRUCTIONS FOR COOKING PASTA

HOW TO COOK PASTA

The Classical Method

1 lb pasta   1–2 tablespoons ($1\frac{1}{4}$–$2\frac{1}{2}$) salt
8 pints (10) water

1 Use a large saucepan.
2 Fill with water. (Never cook pasta in too little water, if you do it will stick.) Bring the water to a rapid, bubbling boil, then add the salt.
3 Add the pasta all at once. If using long pasta, do not break it, fan it out and gently ease it into the pan. Stir well with a three-pronged fork for long pasta, a smaller fork for smaller shapes. Cover the pan and let it cook for a few seconds until the water is rapidly boiling again.
4 When the water is boiling again, stir the pasta and continue boiling without the lid for the time indicated on the package. Stir from time to time.
5 Do not over-cook.
6 Drain the pasta at once in a colander. Do not drain too thoroughly as the pasta is greedy for water and should remain just a little moist. This moisture, which is like a thin film over the pasta, disappears rapidly.
7 DO NOT ON ANY ACCOUNT RINSE IT IN COLD WATER, this results only in chilled pasta and no amount of hot sauce will make it hot. Pasta should always be served hot, unless in a salad.
8 The pasta can be turned into a hot serving dish after draining but, if using a stove-to-table pan (which is the best way in which

to cook and serve pasta and keep it piping hot), return the pasta at once to the hot pan. Add the sauce, stir it well but gently into the pasta and serve at once.

A New Method of Cooking Pasta

This new, economical method of cooking pasta has been evolved by Eva Agnesi.

1 Have the water boiling rapidly as in the classical method, and well salted.

2 Add the pasta. Cook fine pasta for 2 minutes, thick shapes for 3 minutes. Stir well. Wrap the saucepan lid in a cloth and cover the pan tightly. Immediately turn off the heat and leave the pasta in the water for the exact cooking time given on the package. For example, if cooking gnocchi, first cook for 3 minutes with the heat on, then leave covered without heat for 11 minutes.

3 Drain, not too much, leaving a thin film of water on the pasta.

4 Dress with the chosen sauce and serve at once.

The point of this method is that it is consistently good and the pasta is more elastic. Also, you save fuel. Most important, however, the pasta liquid remains almost clear, and is proof that the pasta has retained its rich content of vitamins, minerals and micro-elements, instead of dissolving them in the water.

Another point in favour of this method (which I use all the time, except for soups or when pasta requires only 3 minutes in all to cook) is that if one should leave the pasta a minute or so over its cooking time it won't become soggy as it will when cooked the traditional way.

If using an electric cooker which takes time to cool when turned off, take the pan from the ring as soon as the lid is clamped on the pot, otherwise the water will continue boiling and probably boil over.

How to Cook Lasagne or Wide Pasta Squares

One pound of lasagne is usually sufficient for 4–6 persons.

1 Have ready a large pan with plenty of boiling salted water. Add 1 tablespoon (1¼) of olive oil or butter.

2 Thoroughly wet a clean white cloth with warm water and squeeze it until just damp. Spread this on the kitchen table.

3 Drop 3–4 squares of lasagne into the pan at a time, the size of pasta varies, as do the shapes. If the pan is very large and the pasta squares are not too big, then 6–7 pieces may be cooked at one time. Over-crowding the pot results in the pasta sticking together. The time taken for cooking pasta squares varies according to the type. It varies from 10 to 15 minutes, so consult the package in which it was bought. As the pasta squares cook, they rise to the surface of the water. Take out carefully with a slotted spoon and place each one separately on the damp cloth to drain.

The Boiling – 'Al Dente'

Al dente is an Italian term which literally means 'to the bite' or cooked to a state when you can get your teeth into it. 'Biteable' might be the best translation. To be *al dente*, the pasta must be neither too soft nor too hard. Mushy pasta is not nice to eat, and if pasta is too firm it is probably also somewhat raw.

People vary in most things and not least in taste. Even in Italy there are different opinions as to what constitutes *al dente*. What is worth knowing is that the degree of softness has nothing to do with whether or not the pasta will be more or less digestible.

So how do we determine the exact cooking time?

Certainly we don't need to follow the amusing advice given in one book for beginners: 'When we were young we knew some Italian families who had a fascinating method of testing their spaghetti. The mother would take a few lengths of the spaghetti on a fork and hurl them at the wall over the sink. If the spaghetti stuck to the wall, it was done.' This is one way to test for *al dente*; but while the operation is carried out, the rest of the spaghetti is probably over-cooking.

It is difficult to give exact cooking times for pasta. Different shapes and qualities take different times. Tubular pasta, like macaronis, take a shorter time, for the boiling water runs through them. In other words cooking time is decided by the thickness of the wall of pasta and so it happens that some tiny shapes take a surprisingly long time because they are solid.

To be on the safe side, it is as well to taste pasta after it has been cooking for about three-quarters of the prescribed time. Fish out a strand or shape and bite it. It should feel slightly resistant, a little elastic and the inside should be slightly darker than the outside.

The cooking time given on a packet of pasta should be observed. This has been arrived at through laboratory tests and is determined by the quality of the wheat. However, a word of caution. As in all cooking, times can be affected by such things as the hardness of water, the height above sea level and the diversity of stoves.

Light Draining

Pasta, especially that made with pure durum wheat, takes a lot of water. It will increase three times its volume when cooked. Other pastas, those made with either a mixture of durum and ordinary wheat, or pasta made from mixed flour, expand much less dramatically but still be sure to use plenty of water.

Light draining does not mean that pasta should be served swimming in water, simply that it should be left slightly moist. If it is too well drained, it will become dry and tacky.

Neapolitans, who know a lot about pasta, take it out of the water with a big fork, then drop the trickling spaghetti on to the individual plates. This way there is a veil of water on each plate, which is absorbed by the time the pasta has been eaten. In Sicily, the pasta is drained through a colander and then put into a central dish, but a small pot of the pasta liquid is often placed on the table by it.

The Water

The best water in which to cook pasta is *acqua dolce*, that is soft or sweet water. And the best salt to use is bay or sea salt. Some of the highly refined salts, especially those which contain calcium, will actually harden the water and pasta is not as good cooked in hard water as in soft.

Apart from salt, some cooks advise adding a tablespoonful of olive oil to the water in which they are cooking pasta. This is said to prevent the pasta from sticking. In my experience it is a real help when cooking a very large pasta, especially pasta squares, but not necessary for the smaller shapes, or long pasta, where plenty of water and the occasional stir are all that is needed.

Quantities

Unless otherwise stated, the number of servings for the recipes in this book is from four to six. It is not easy to be exact as so much depends on appetite and on whether the pasta is to be served as a main dish or to start a meal. Allowing four to six portions for one pound of pasta allows a fair margin.

Apart from appetites, pasta varies. One increases in volume more than another and one therefore eats less of it. Certainly one pound of pasta will not serve more than six people, and those with hearty appetites will want more.

With baked dishes, because of the many side ingredients, $\frac{1}{2}$ lb of pasta will serve four to six. In left-over dishes, when a recipe calls for $\frac{1}{2}$ lb of cooked macaroni, this is the cooked weight.

Oven Cooking

All ovens should be pre-heated before the food is put in. This also applies to grills and even to the frying pan in which fat or oil is to be heated. Always make sure when frying that the fat is really hot before you begin otherwise whatever you are frying will become soggy instead of being crisp outside and tender inside as it should be.

How to Serve and Eat Pasta

Pasta must be served immediately it is cooked. Like a soufflé, it cannot wait. It should be served on hot plates.

I use a bright-red pasta pot which is elegant enough to bring to the table and drain my pasta quickly into a colander so that when I return the hot pasta to the emptied pasta pot, a good deal of the liquid is still clinging to the sides. Then the pasta is either brought to the table as it is, and the sauce served separately, or the sauce is added in the pot and stirred quickly but very gently into the pasta.

The best type of plates in which to serve pasta are rather deep ones with sloping sides, similar but not identical to the average soup plate.

There is an art in the eating of spaghetti as well as in its cooking. Most Italians use a fork, without the help of a spoon, and never, never a knife. There is the story of the foreigner in Genoa who, lunching with some Italian friends, attacked his spaghetti with a knife, cutting it into little pieces. His hostess flung her arms up in the air and cried out 'Assassin'.

The most efficient technique is to wind the pasta lengths, not too many at a time, around the tines of the fork but be careful not to allow any rebellious strands to wind round the neck of the fork. Remember that you are allowed to twist them round the inside of the plate, hence the preference for a sloping edge, but whatever you do, don't let the pasta get cold in the process, for this is to commit the worst sin in the spaghetti gourmet book.

Pasta Shapes

Some say there are thousands of different pasta shapes, a claim as sensational as the Arabs' that there are as many *pilaus* as there are stars in the sky. The less colourful truth is that there are, in Italy, between 150 and 200 shapes and about 600 different names.

One might well ask, why so many different shapes? Well, Italians eat pasta every day, sometimes twice a day, and they like to have a change. So it is that we have our little bows and butter-flies, elephant's teeth and angel's hair.

An Italian cookery writer wrote: 'The Italians couldn't possibly give cold, unfeeling numbers or simple descriptive names to macaroni.' And this being so they culled names from every sphere of daily life to enrich the world of pasta with gay superlatives.

What are these shapes? First, there are all the various strings, i.e. spaghetti and the rest of that family. Then there is a myriad of flat noodles of all widths. There is the thin, positively hair-thin 'capelli d'angelo', angel's hair, coming sometimes in lengths, sometimes in hanks, 'matasse'. There are the long and short tubes, some smooth, some ridged, some large, like mezze maniche, or millerighe of which two or three stuffed will make a meal. There are large and small squares for baked dishes or to turn into cannelloni. Quite different from these are the tiny pastina, used in soups, baby dishes, also in desserts (see page 141).

The names given to these shapes are curious. Why should a fat strip of pasta be called 'zita', or bride? Or perhaps, why not? Some shapes, like 'stelline', little stars, look like stars. Elephant's teeth, 'denti d'elefante', are long and slightly curved, but why are little shells called 'chinesi'? The word means Chinese. But often the names are pet names from the fertile imagination of the manufacturers.

The next question could be, do the different shapes have different flavours? The answer is, yes. But how can one explain this difference? It is not marked but it is there. Sometimes it has to do with the cooking. For instance, thicker shapes are not always cooked right through. The Italians like it this way. Those who prefer to over-cook their pasta a shade, will get a slightly different flavour to the *al dente* taste, some say it is better. One way in which to discover pasta flavours is to taste the pasta first without a sauce, or perhaps simply with unsalted butter.

It is generally agreed that some sauces go better with flat noodles than with round shapes. The clam, 'vongole', sauces go better with bucatini than with other pasta; wide noodles take to Bolognese sauce and Pesto better than round shapes. Spaghetti and meat balls seem to go together, and, of course, narrow, flat noodles and butter (with or without cheese) is a natural.

The recipes in this book have been grouped according to their various shapes. All the spaghettis are together with the long and short strings. Under noodles are included all the flat lengths, whether they come in lengths or hanks (*in matasse*), or wide and square as for lasagne and cannelloni. Under macaroni shapes I have included most of the large, fancy shapes.

There are five main groups, as follows:

1 Those used for boiling: thin strings of pasta such as spaghetti; spaghettini; vermicelli; bucatini; guitar (spaghetti alla chittarra), and the various hanks of pasta, plus many of the narrow noodles.
2 Those which are both boiled and baked: the tubular forms, all the macaronis, and the thicker fancy shapes, such as zita, penne rigate, and denti d'elefante.
3 Flat pasta: such as the wider noodles, lasagne squares, etc.
4 Fancy shapes.
5 Envelopes of stuffed pasta with which we are not concerned in this book as it deals with commercially or industrially produced pasta dishes only.

The full range of pasta shapes is not usually found outside Italy but with the growing interest in pasta dishes it is increasing at a spectacular rate both in Britain and in the United States. Much of the pasta that is sold throughout the world is Italian – although other countries do make and export it too – and it is for this reason that I have chosen to give the Italian names for the pasta shapes. When a particular shape cannot be found, choose a similar one, using the list displayed on the endpapers of this book as a guide. Many shapes are interchangeable.

I feel I must mention Pasta Gemma which is an extra fine pasta in which the whole of the wheat germ has been retained. This is a pasta for the connoisseur. It is slightly more expensive than the general run of pasta and comes in one shape only, the long spaghetti shape, but, like a vintage wine, it is well worth the extra money.

Pasta With or Without Eggs?

If industrially-prepared pasta is made with durum wheat, eggs are superfluous. Durum wheat provides sufficient protein and without eggs the pasta has a much longer life.

But tradition dies hard. Pasta made at home required eggs to bind the plain flour and water – home-made pasta cannot be made with durum wheat which needs a heavy machine to bind it – so people accustomed to home-made pasta came to believe that eggs are necessary to good pasta, and think industrial pasta too should have eggs.

Somewhere along the line it became fashionable to add eggs even to durum wheat pasta which is rather like adding cream to cream. The public remembers what mother made and chooses to forget that some of her methods are now old-fashioned and may not be applicable to machine-made products.

Finally, and most important, pasta made with eggs does not keep well for eggs when fresh are full of vitamins which if kept too long deteriorate fast. So pasta made with durum wheat but not containing eggs is what we should look for.

Pasta Pointers

It has become a tradition in Britain and America that after pasta has been boiled it should be drained and then rinsed under running water. (I have even read that it should be washed before being used and then again after it has been cooked.)

Pasta that is to be used immediately and with a sauce should NEVER be rinsed. It should be drained and served at once. Rinsing only results in cold, soggy pasta which nothing can be done to improve.

However, when making a dish of baked pasta, this should be very slightly under-cooked, then drained and immersed in a bowl of cold water – not rinsed under running water as the pressure of tap water is usually too strong for the delicate pasta. After the pasta has been rinsed, it must at once be drained and well drained otherwise while you are preparing the rest of the dish the top will become dry and the underneath remain wet and soggy.

If preparing a pasta dish for lunch knowing that perhaps not everyone will arrive on time, the pasta can be boiled in advance but under-cooked, drained, rinsed in cold water, well drained again and put to one side. When ready for cooking, re-boil it for half a minute in rapidly-boiling water. It will be as perfectly cooked as if freshly boiled.

Incidentally, if preparing pasta in this way, do strain off the pasta liquid into a bowl and keep it hot so that it can be used again for the re-boiling.

If for some reason pasta has been cooked, drained and rinsed and then not used, it can be kept in the refrigerator for a day or two without spoiling. However, it can only be used in baked savoury or sweet dishes.

When using long pasta, unless specifically instructed to do so, do not break the lengths. Keep in mind the old Bolognese proverb: long pasta but short bills.

Buying and Storing Pasta

Good quality pasta will keep for a very long time without either losing its flavour or getting stale. Curiously enough, it has been found that fresh packaged pasta, that which comes straight from the factory, does not have such good cooking qualities, it should be at least one month old.

A British doctor of my acquaintance kept some pasta shapes for ten years and found it to be still in good condition.

Generally speaking, however, the normal life-span of pasta, that is without eggs and bran and prepared with durum wheat, is eighteen months to two years. But even up to five years makers guarantee their pasta will still be of good flavour.

Pasta must be stored in a dry place. It does not need to be kept in tins or jars. In fact, it is best kept in its package. Even when a package has been opened, the contents will remain good for a long time, always provided it is kept in a dry place.

Since there is no problem about keeping pasta, except perhaps lack of space, it is wise to buy a number of different shapes at a time. Once one has learnt to cook pasta correctly, to vary the sauces and methods of cooking, and also to use up left-over pasta in appetizing ways, then to have a dozen or more packets in the store cupboard at one time is not excessive. Once you have discovered the make of pasta you like best, keep to this and the cooking will become almost automatic.

How to Recognize Good Pasta
In this book I have continually stressed the importance of using good quality pasta. But how does one tell one from another? Experience quickly teaches that a good brand of pasta differs from an inferior brand, as night from day. The simple answer is, good quality pasta retains the wheat germ while the less good does not. There is the same degree of difference between a grain of wheat retaining its germ and one deprived of it, as between a virile man and a fat eunuch with limp and flabby tissues.

Some Guidelines
1 Good quality pasta should be amber-yellow. Try holding it up against a strong light. It should be translucid and show a clear ground with few spots, not more than two or three for each length of spaghetti. If there are more spots, they are probably bran which gives the cooked pasta an almost harsh flavour. If there are just a few spots, these are probably the wheat germ.
2 The cooking test: pasta made with the best quality durum wheat has good cooking qualities. After it has been cooked to *al dente*, you will find the surface smooth, the pasta evenly cooked throughout and not at all sticky.

1. Sweet Macaroni Pudding

2. Spaghetti with Tunny Fish

3 Test of taste: good quality pasta has a sweet taste, almost nut-like. It is a good idea to try it without adding sauce, maybe just with a little butter. It is also a good test to sip the water in which it was cooked. If the pasta was good, then the water in which it was cooked will have a good clean smell – and can be used as a soup basis. Poor quality pasta produces a water with a coarse, even harsh taste; this is because of the bran content.

4 Test of volume increase: a good pasta will increase to three times its volume in cooking. This is due to the protein content (14 to 15 per cent in the best quality pasta). Obviously this means that the extra cost of buying good quality pasta is repaid since you require less pasta per person.

5 Test of water consumption: good pasta continues to absorb water even when it is on the plate. Before you eat your spaghetti, push it a little on one side, pick it up with a fork and you will see if the pasta has been correctly drained, that is, not over-drained. There should be a thin film of water at the bottom of the plate. By the time you have eaten the pasta, this water will have disappeared, it will have been absorbed by the pasta, if the pasta is made from durum wheat.

MAIN INGREDIENTS USED IN COOKING PASTA

1 *Olive Oil*

I have suggested using olive oil in all of the following recipes but there is no need to follow this advice blindly. Olive oil is expensive, even in those areas where it is produced. I like to use olive oil in cooking, above all the mild sweet oil of Liguria, but it is a matter of taste. There are several qualities of olive oil. Some people prefer an oil with a heavy flavour, others something more delicate. When buying olive oil, if possible buy pure virgin oil. When you buy refined oil you are getting the second or even the third pressing of the olives. However, many people have become used to this flavour and they prefer it.

There are many other good cooking oils, all of which can be used in cooking pasta. Peanut or groundnut oil is a favourite with many cooks; it is light and does not have too strong a flavour. Walnut oil has a particularly delicate flavour and is even more popular than olive oil in certain parts of France. But it isn't cheap. There are also various vegetable oils, corn oil, sesame and sunflower oils. Any of these can be used according to what pleases both the taste buds and the pocket.

2 Cooking Fats
Butter is used in the following recipes, preferably unsalted. But this, as with the oil, is a matter of choice, taste and pocket. Some people are not allowed to eat butter, others prefer vegetable fats, dripping or chicken fat. All these can be used instead of unsalted butter though they will produce a slightly different flavour.

3 Cheese
Although we usually associate Parmesan with pasta dishes, there is no reason at all why other hard, well-flavoured cheeses should not be used instead. Parmesan is dear, even in Italy. There are some classic Italian pasta dishes in which it would be a pity not to use Parmesan but, generally speaking, any good, hard cheese will do.

What is most important is that you grate the cheese at home. There are several excellent gadgets for grating cheese on the market, and the job only takes a matter of minutes. Buying a chunk of cheese and grating it oneself is infinitely better than relying on a cheese which has been grated heaven-knows how long ago and has lost all its freshness and flavour. It is also cheaper to do it this way.

4 Cream Cheese
The term 'cream cheese' is used to describe all soft cheeses. The variety called for in these recipes is curd cheese, which can be bought in most large food stores and delicatessens. It is better bought fresh and by the weight than in boxes. Italian stores sell Ricotta, a firm, dry curd or whey cheese which is one of the best cream cheeses to use in cooking.

5 Tomatoes
For a tomato sauce, red, very ripe tomatoes are the best. Fortunately canned tomatoes are almost as good as fresh ones,

so when fresh tomatoes are expensive, use these. If you want to get an authentic Italian flavour to your sauce, use Italian canned tomatoes; if it is, say, a Balkan flavour you seek, then buy Balkan tomatoes. Tomatoes from different countries do have their own flavour.

Tomato paste is usually bought canned (though those with a blender naturally can make their own). It must be dissolved in water before being used, just enough to make it workable, but not turned into a tomato drink.

6 Dried Mushrooms

These are a useful addition to any larder. Before using, they must be soaked in tepid water for 20 minutes. They do not require long cooking, anything between 5 to 15 minutes. If cooked too long, they lose their flavour. When buying dried mushrooms, choose those which are a creamy colour. Those which look black and are gnarled are old.

7 Breadcrumbs

These can be bought ready-made, and some are better than others. However, in these days of blenders, breadcrumbs are very easy to make. The bread can be oven-dried and blended, or excellent fine breadcrumbs can be made with rusks or other dry, plain biscuits. Breadcrumbs, provided they are made from oven-dried bread, will keep some time in an air-tight tin. Fresh bread-crumbs keep only for a few days and are best made as and when required.

8 Herbs

These are important in all cooking, at least for savoury dishes and especially when flavouring a sauce, stew or soup. It is not always easy either to grow or buy fresh herbs, which is a great pity for dried herbs, no matter how well dried, are never quite the same. However, they are better than no herbs at all and should be bought in small quantities as once the package in which they were sealed is opened they quickly go stale.

In the following recipes various fresh herbs are called for. They are worth trying to obtain for naturally they make a difference to the finished dish. But, if you cannot get them, do not despair. Buy and use what is available.

Incidentally, if you come across Continental or flat-leafed parsley, this is worth trying for its flavour is milder and more subtle than the curly-leafed variety.

9 *Spices*

Pepper and nutmeg are the two main spices used in pasta cooking and should always be freshly ground or grated.

CHAPTER TWO

SOUPS

'Pastina' is the overall name for the smallest of the pasta shapes, some so small one wonders how the machines can produce them. These shapes often have the most fanciful names. For instance, 'avemaria', which is so named because the little shapes resemble the small bead of a rosary, or 'stellette' meaning little star. All the shapes mentioned in the following recipes can be found illustrated on the endpapers of this book.

SWISS SOUP

3 oz (¾ cup) anellini
3 pints (scant 4) half milk, half
   chicken stock
salt and pepper to taste

1 egg yolk, well beaten
pinch nutmeg
½ oz (1 tablespoon) butter

Combine milk and stock, bring to the boil and season. Add the anellini and cook until tender (11 minutes). Take ½ cupful of the soup and whisk into the egg yolk. Add nutmeg. Take the pan from the stove. Stir the egg yolk mixture into the boiling soup. Add the butter, stir until it has melted and serve at once.

EGG AND CHEESE SOUP WITH PISELLINI

3 oz (¾ cup) pisellini
3 pints (scant 4) meat or chicken
   stock
salt and pepper to taste
1 egg, well beaten

2 tablespoons (2½) grated Parmesan
   cheese
½ clove garlic, minced
pinch dried oregano or marjoram

Bring the stock to the boil, season, add the pisellini, stir, lower the heat and cook until tender (14 minutes). Beat the egg, cheese, garlic and oregano together. Dilute with a little of the boiling stock. Take the pan from the stove, add the egg mixture, stirring vigorously. Serve at once.

CHICKEN AND ONION SOUP WITH PUNTETTE

3 oz (¾ cup) puntette
3 pints (scant 4) chicken stock
1 onion, minced

½ oz (1 tablespoon) butter
salt and pepper to taste
grated cheese to taste

Heat the butter and add 2 tablespoonfuls (2½) of water. Put in the onion, and cook gently for 5 minutes. Add the stock, stir, bring to the boil, season and stir in the puntette. Cook for 19 minutes, stirring from time to time. Serve sprinkled with cheese.

SOUP BELLE HÉLÈNE

3 oz (¾ cup) occhi di pernice
3 pints (scant 4) chicken stock
salt
1 tablespoon (1¼) minced parsley

2 oz (½ cup) diced Bel Paese
cheese
pinch each nutmeg and pepper
1 tablespoon (1¼) brandy

Cook the occhi di pernice in boiling salted stock for 10 minutes. Add the parsley and cheese and stir until the cheese has melted. Take from the stove. Add nutmeg, pepper and brandy. Serve at once.
      Other clear soup stock can be used in the same way.

CAULIFLOWER SOUP WITH AVEMARIA

3 oz (¾ cup) avemaria
1 small green cauliflower or broccoli
½ lb potatoes, peeled and diced
1 onion, chopped

3 tablespoons (3¾) olive oil
salt to taste
½ oz (1 tablespoon) butter
grated cheese to taste

Put the potatoes and onion into a pan with 4 pints (5) of water, add the oil and salt. Cook over a moderate heat. Break the cauliflower into flowerets, add to the pan and cook until just tender. Add the avemaria, stir well and cook for 14 minutes. Take from the stove, add the butter and cheese, stir well and serve.

COURGETTE SOUP WITH STELLETTE

3 oz (¾ cup) stellette
1 lb courgettes (zucchini), thinly sliced
½ oz (1 tablespoon) butter
2 tablespoons (2½) olive oil
1 onion, thinly sliced

3 pints (scant 4) clear stock
salt and pepper to taste
1 egg, well beaten
2 tablespoons (2½) grated cheese
1 tablespoon (1¼) minced parsley

Heat the butter, oil and ½ cupful of water in a large pan. Add the onion and courgettes and cook for 15 minutes. Add the stock, bring to the boil, season, add the stellette and stir. Cook until tender (19 minutes), stirring occasionally. Combine the egg, cheese and parsley, add a little stock, and pour this mixture into the soup, stirring vigorously to prevent the egg from curdling. Serve at once.

GREEN PEA SOUP WITH DITALINI

3 oz (¾ cup) ditalini
1 lb peas, shelled, frozen or canned
1 tablespoon (1¼) olive oil
1 large onion, minced
4 pints (5) boiling meat stock

salt to taste
4–5 sprigs parsley, minced
½ oz (1 tablespoon) butter
grated cheese to taste

Heat the oil, add the onion and ½ cupful of stock, bring to the boil, add the peas and cook until almost tender. Now add the remaining stock, salt and ditalini, stir frequently and continue cooking for 9 minutes. Add the parsley, stir well and cook for another 2 minutes. Remove from the stove, add the butter and cheese, stir until the butter has melted, and serve.

BEAN SOUP WITH CHIFFERINI RIGATI

¼ lb chifferini rigati
1 cup (1¼) dried red or white beans, soaked overnight
6 tablespoons (½ cup) olive oil

1 small onion, sliced
1 small carrot, sliced
1 small ham bone
salt and pepper to taste

Heat half the oil with ½ cupful of water, add the onion and carrot and cook for 5 minutes. Add the ham bone and the beans, with their liquid, plus enough water to make 5 pints (6¼). Cook over a low heat until the beans are just tender. Remove the ham bone. Add the salt, raise the heat, then add the chifferini rigati. Cook for 12 minutes. Immediately before serving, add the remaining oil and pepper.

Instead of dried beans, canned beans may be used. They should be well drained and added after the ham bone has been cooking for 30 minutes. Less liquid will be needed as the long cooking required with dried beans greatly reduces the original quantity.

ONION AND POTATO SOUP WITH CHINESINI

3 oz (1 cup) chinesini
2 large onions, sliced
¾ lb potatoes, diced
3 tablespoons (3¾) olive oil

salt and pepper to taste
pinch dried marjoram
grated cheese to taste

Heat the oil with a cupful of water, add the onions and cook for 2 minutes. Add the potatoes and 4 pints (5) of boiling water. Season. Cook over a moderate heat for 20 minutes. Add the chinesini and cook another 13 minutes. Add the marjoram and stir. Serve at once, with the cheese separately.

MACARONI SOUP

3 oz (1 cup) pennini
3 pints (scant 4) meat or chicken
  stock

salt and pepper

Cook the pennini in boiling salted water as described on page 23 but for 2 minutes less than the prescribed time. While you are doing this bring the stock to the boil. Drain the pennini and throw it at once into the boiling stock. Cook rapidly for another 2 minutes. Test for seasoning. Add salt and pepper to taste.

ANGEL'S HAIR SOUP

$\frac{1}{4}$ lb capelli d'angelo
3 pints (scant 4) clear stock
1 egg

1 tablespoon ($1\frac{1}{4}$) lemon juice
salt and pepper (optional)

Bring the stock to the boil. Add the capelli d'angelo and cook for 2 minutes. Stir well, beat the egg thoroughly, add the lemon juice and 1 tablespoon ($1\frac{1}{4}$) of hot stock. Pour this into the soup. Stir well and serve. Salt and pepper may be added but taste the stock first.

Capelli d'angelo in hanks can be cooked in the same way.

ANGEL'S HAIR SOUP WITH EGGS
AND CHEESE

$\frac{1}{4}$ lb capelli d'angelo
salt
2 eggs

$1\frac{1}{2}$ oz (scant $\frac{1}{2}$ cup) grated cheese
1 oz (2 tablespoons) butter,
  softened

Break the capelli d'angelo into short lengths and cook in 3 pints (scant 4) of boiling salted water for 2 minutes. Beat the eggs with the cheese and butter. Beat in 2–3 tablespoonfuls of the liquid in which the capelli d'angelo is cooking. Immediately before serving, add the egg and cheese mixture and beat lightly.

Instead of water, a clear meat or chicken stock may be used.

TORTELLINI IN CONSOMMÉ OR CLEAR STOCK

½ lb tortellini (see below)   salt and pepper
3 pints (scant 4) stock or consommé   grated cheese

Bring the stock or consommé to a rapid boil and test for seasoning before adding salt and pepper. Add the tortellini and cook them for the time recommended on the package. Serve with grated cheese.

Tortellini are tiny, stuffed pasta in the shape of a navel and there are three stories as to the origin of this shape.

One version is that a famous cook in Modena dreamt one night that he saw Venus arising from the sea. As he glimpsed her perfect navel he awoke and at once rushed into his kitchen to recreate such perfection in the only way he could express himself, by rolling up a small piece of pasta in the form of a navel.

Another story has it that Venus spent the night at an inn in Bologna and her beauty inspired the innkeeper, who was also the cook. While Venus was sleeping, naked as the gods were wont to do, the innkeeper crept upstairs and peeped through the keyhole. Alas, all he could see was the famous navel. So, disappointed but still with the instinct of the natural cook unimpaired, he went to his kitchen and, taking up a batch of pasta, shaped it into those small navel-like shapes we know as tortellini.

The last story, more prosaic and more likely true, is that the cook working in a small inn fell in love with his employer's lovely wife. She too slept naked and the love-hungry cook who crept up to her bedroom door was rewarded only with the sight of her navel. The rest of the story is as above.

Tortellini are still made at home, in the better inns and restaurants and also in the fresh pasta stores, where they come off small machines which are fascinating to watch. They also are sold frozen.

Bologna is the city which claims to have invented this pasta shape and has a society called the Learned Order of the Tortellini.

CHAPTER THREE

FISH

SPAGHETTI WITH ANCHOVY SAUCE

1 lb spaghetti (bucatini)
8–12 anchovy fillets
½ cup (⅔) olive oil

1½ cups (2) coarsely-ground soft
  breadcrumbs
chilli or cayenne pepper

Heat half the oil, add the anchovies and cook, stirring all the time, until they are dissolved. Put aside but keep warm. Heat the remaining oil in another pan and fry the breadcrumbs until brown. Sprinkle with plenty of chilli or cayenne pepper, put them into a warm bowl and keep warm.

Cook the spaghetti in boiling salted water as described on page 23. Drain and return it to the hot pan or turn into a deep dish and stir in the anchovy sauce. Serve the fried breadcrumbs separately.

SPAGHETTI WITH ANCHOVY AND TUNNY FISH SAUCE

1 lb spaghetti
8 anchovy fillets
1 small can tunny (tuna) fish
olive oil
1 medium-sized can peeled
  tomatoes, chopped

salt
1 teaspoon (1¼) sugar (optional)
12 black olives, pitted and chopped
¼ lb soft cheese, diced
pepper

Heat 3 tablespoons (3¾) of oil, add the tomatoes with a little salt and the sugar. Cook over a brisk heat for 15 minutes. Pound the

44

anchovies together in a mortar with the tunny and olives, or purée in a blender. If using a blender, add 2–3 tablespoonfuls of oil to the mixture at the same time. Gradually add enough oil to make a thick paste, like a mayonnaise. Gently heat the paste but do not let it boil.

Cook the spaghetti in boiling salted water as described on page 23. Drain, return to the pan or turn it into a hot serving dish and at once stir in the tomato sauce, the anchovy and tunny paste, the cheese and pepper. Serve at once.

SPAGHETTI SAILOR'S STYLE

1 lb spaghetti
6 tablespoons (7½) olive oil
1–2 onions, finely chopped
1–2 cloves garlic
2 lb canned peeled tomatoes, chopped

1 teaspoon (1¼) sugar
6–8 anchovy fillets
1 tablespoon (1¼) finely-chopped parsley
1 cup (1¼) grated cheese

Heat the oil, add the onion and garlic and cook over a moderate heat until the onion changes colour. Discard the garlic. Add the tomatoes, sugar and anchovies and cook over a moderate heat for 15–20 minutes.

While the sauce is cooking, cook the spaghetti in boiling salted water as described on page 23. Drain and return it to the hot saucepan or turn it into a hot serving dish. Sprinkle with the parsley and 2 tablespoons (2½) of the cheese. Then add the sauce, stirring quickly but gently. Serve the rest of the cheese separately.

SPAGHETTI WITH CLAMS

1 lb spaghetti (bucatini or linguine)
½ lb shelled clams, frozen or fresh
2–3 tablespoons (2½–3¾) olive oil
2 cloves garlic, chopped
1 small onion, finely chopped

1 lb ripe tomatoes, peeled and chopped
salt and pepper
2–3 sprigs parsley, finely chopped

Heat the oil, add the garlic and onion and cook gently until the onion begins to change colour. Add the tomatoes and the liquid from the clams (even if using frozen clams). Add salt and pepper and cook over a brisk heat for 20 minutes.

While the sauce is cooking, cook the spaghetti in boiling salted water as described on page 23. Just before draining the spaghetti, add the clams and parsley to the tomato sauce and cook for 1 minute. Drain the spaghetti, return it to the hot pan or turn it into a hot dish, stir in the clam and tomato sauce and serve at once.

BAKED SPAGHETTI WITH CRAB MEAT

½ lb spaghetti
1 medium-sized can crab meat
½ pint (1¼ cups) Béchamel sauce
  (see page 138)

¼ lb grated hard cheese
pepper

Cook the spaghetti in boiling salted water as described on page 23. Drain and rinse quickly in cold water.

Make the Béchamel sauce. Stir in three-quarters of the grated cheese (leave some to sprinkle on top of the dish when served). Combine the cheese sauce with the spaghetti and crab meat and season with pepper. Place in a greased, shallow baking dish and bake in a moderate oven (350°F., mark 4) for 20–25 minutes. Serve sprinkled with the remaining cheese.

Other fish, i.e. salmon, lobster and tunny (tuna) can be cooked in the same way.

SPAGHETTI WITH MUSSELS OR CLAMS

1 lb spaghetti
½ lb frozen mussels or clams
½ cup (⅔) olive oil

1 clove garlic, finely chopped
2–3 sprigs parsley, finely chopped
pepper

Heat the oil, fry and brown the garlic, add the mussels or clams
with their juice, the parsley and pepper. Cook over a low heat for
5 minutes, no longer or the fish will toughen.

Cook the spaghetti in boiling salted water and drain as described on page 23. Return it to the pan or turn into a hot dish
and stir in the sauce.

SPAGHETTI WITH CANNED SALMON

½ lb spaghetti (spaghettini)
½–¾ lb can salmon
1 large can cream of asparagus
   soup
½ pint (1¼ cups) milk
a few green olives, stoned

a good pinch dried marjoram
salt and pepper
1 teaspoon (1¼) onion salt
fine breadcrumbs and butter for
   garnishing

Cook the spaghetti in boiling salted water as described on page
23 and while it is cooking combine the remaining ingredients,
except the garnish, and bring gently to the boil in a large saucepan.
Drain the spaghetti, turn it into the sauce and then pour into a
large, deep casserole. Sprinkle generously with breadcrumbs and
dot with slivers of butter. Bake in a moderate oven (350°F., mark
4) for 30 minutes or until the top is brown.

SPAGHETTI WITH SARDINE AND OLIVE SAUCE

1 lb spaghetti
4–6 canned sardines, boned and
   crumbled

20 small black olives, stoned and
   chopped
5 tablespoons (6¼) olive oil
grated cheese to taste

Cook the spaghetti in boiling salted water as described on
page 23. Heat the oil, add the sardines and cook until dissolved.

Add the olives and stir. Drain the spaghetti, return it to the pan or turn it into a hot dish, add the sauce, stir lightly and sprinkle with cheese. Serve at once.

SPAGHETTI WITH SHRIMP SAUCE

1 lb spaghetti (bucatini or linguine)
½–¾ lb cooked shelled shrimps or
  small prawns
1 oz (2 tablespoons) butter
1 clove garlic, crushed
1 stalk celery, chopped

1 small green sweet pepper, cored,
  seeded and chopped
1 oz (2 tablespoons) plain flour
salt and pepper
1 cup (1¼) milk
grated cheese (optional)

Cook the spaghetti in boiling salted water as described on page 23. While it is cooking, prepare the sauce. Heat the butter, add the garlic and as soon as it is brown remove and discard. Add the celery and sweet pepper. Add the flour and stir this well into the butter. Add salt and pepper. Gradually add the milk, stirring continuously. Cook over a low heat for about 15 minutes. Add the shrimps and cook only long enough to heat – if they are over-cooked they become tough.

Drain the spaghetti and return it to the pan, add the sauce, mix well and serve at once. Serve the cheese separately.

Instead of milk, a fish stock with wine, beer or cider may be used.

Note: frozen or canned shellfish may be used if fresh are not available and peas or asparagus tips can be substituted for celery and green pepper.

SPAGHETTI WITH TUNNY FISH

1 lb spaghetti
1 medium-sized can tunny (tuna)
  fish
2 tablespoons (2½) olive oil
1 clove garlic, crushed

1 large can peeled tomatoes
salt and pepper
½ teaspoon (⅔) dried oregano or
  marjoram

Heat the oil, fry the garlic until brown and then discard it. Add the tomatoes, salt and pepper and cook over a good heat for 20 minutes. Flake the fish with a fork, stir it gently into the tomatoes, add the oregano, stir well, reduce the heat and cook for about 10 minutes.

Cook the spaghetti in boiling salted water as described on page 23. Drain, return to the pan or turn it into a hot serving dish. Stir in the hot sauce, toss lightly and serve at once.

Canned salmon can be used instead of tunny.

MACARONI IN PRAWN (SHRIMP) SAUCE

1 lb macaroni (chifferotti or
    chifferoni)
1 lb cooked shelled small prawns
    or shrimps
¼ cup (⅓) olive oil
2 large onions, minced
1–2 green or red sweet peppers

1 clove garlic, minced
1 large can peeled tomatoes, sieved
dried coarsely-chopped chillies to
    taste
salt to taste
1 teaspoon (1¼) sugar

Heat the oil in a large pan. Add the onions, peppers* and garlic and cook over a moderate heat for 10 minutes. Add the sieved tomatoes, chillies, salt and sugar, stir well into the onions and peppers and, over a gentle heat, continue cooking for 30 minutes. Stir from time to time.

While the sauce is cooking, prepare the macaroni as described on page 23. About 1–2 minutes before the macaroni is drained, add the prawns or shrimps to the pan. Remember that if they are cooked too long they will become tough. When the macaroni is *al dente*, drain, add to the sauce, stir gently and serve at once.

* When coring the peppers, remember to remove all the seeds as they are usually very hot. The chillies should be quite sufficient to give this dish its characteristic pepper-hot flavour.

MACARONI WITH ANCHOVY AND GARLIC SAUCE

6 servings:

1 lb macaroni (lumaconi)
6 anchovy fillets
2 cloves garlic, crushed
½ cup (⅔) olive oil
2 oz (½ cup) butter
a few fennel seeds

plenty fresh parsley, finely chopped
1 small onion, finely chopped
½ pint (1¼ cups) dry white wine,
   dry cider or beer
pepper
grated nutmeg

Cook the macaroni in boiling salted water as described on page 23. While it is cooking, make the sauce. Heat the oil and butter together in a large pan, add the garlic, let this brown, take it out and discard. Add the anchovies, fennel seeds, parsley and onion and cook gently until the onion browns.

Drain the macaroni, turn at once into the pan with the still-simmering sauce, stir it well, add the wine, a good sprinkling of pepper and nutmeg, and stir with a fork until the macaroni is completely covered with the sauce. Serve at once.

Other small, thick pasta also can be used with this sauce.

BAKED MACARONI AND CANNED SALMON CUSTARD

½ lb macaroni (abissini or gnocchi)
1½-lb can salmon
2 oz (4 tablespoons) butter or margarine
1 oz (2 tablespoons) plain flour
1 pint (2½ cups) milk
salt and pepper

1 canned or bottled pimento, chopped (optional)
2 eggs, separated
1 tablespoon (1¼) minced parsley
butter for greasing
1 small can peas or asparagus tips

Cook the macaroni in boiling salted water as described on page 23. While it is cooking, make the sauce. Drain and flake the salmon. Melt the butter, add the flour and stir until the mixture is smooth. Gradually add the milk, stirring all the time. When the sauce is thick, add salt, pepper and pimento. Take from the heat and put aside 1 cupful of the sauce. Beat the egg yolks, one at a time, into the remaining sauce. Beat the mixture thoroughly.

Drain the macaroni. Fold this into the sauce with the egg yolks, add the parsley and salmon. Beat the egg whites until stiff but not dry. Fold into the macaroni-salmon mixture using a metal spoon.

Rub a round baking dish (a soufflé dish is ideal) with butter. Add the macaroni-salmon mixture. Put into a baking pan with hot water and bake in a slow oven (325°F., mark 3) for 1 hour.

Drain the peas or asparagus tips and combine with the reserved sauce. Gently reheat a few minutes before the custard is ready. Serve the custard hot with the peas or asparagus sauce.

If preferred, frozen peas or asparagus tips may be used.

BAKED MACARONI WITH FISH

½ lb macaroni (maccheroni, maccheroni rigati or penne)	2 oz (4 tablespoons) butter
1 lb white fish	½ cup (⅔) cream or milk
salt and pepper	2 eggs, separated
1 bay leaf	grated cheese

Any firm white fish may be used and a little white wine may be added to the liquid in which the fish is cooked. You will need about 1 pint (1¼) of liquid in all.

First gently cook the fish in water, adding salt, pepper and bay leaf. Drain, remove any bones and gently flake the flesh. Put aside until required.

Cook the macaroni in boiling salted water as described on page 23. Drain and mix with the fish. Melt two-thirds of the butter, add salt, pepper, cream and fish stock. Stir and add to the macaroni. Beat the egg yolks until smooth and stir into the macaroni mixture. Finally beat the egg whites until stiff and gently fold into the mixture with a metal spoon. Turn into a baking dish, sprinkle generously with grated cheese, dot with thin slivers of the remaining butter, and bake in a moderate oven (350°F., mark 4) for 30–40 minutes. Serve hot.

MACARONI WITH MUSSELS

½ lb flat noodles (lasagne nidi)
1 pint (1¼) mussels, fresh or frozen
1 pint (1¼) Béchamel sauce (see page 138)

½ pint (1¼ cups) milk
salt
4 well-beaten eggs
fresh parsley, finely chopped
paprika pepper

First make the Béchamel sauce. Put aside but keep warm.

Cook the macaroni in boiling salted water as described on page 23. Drain. Combine with the milk, salt, mussels and eggs and mix well. Put into a large pie dish. Add the Béchamel sauce and lightly mix. Sprinkle with parsley and paprika pepper.

Bake in a moderate oven (350°F., mark 4) for 45 minutes or until set. Serve hot.

LASAGNE WITH PRAWNS OR SHRIMPS

¾–1 lb lasagne squares
1 pint (2½ cups) Béchamel sauce (see page 138)
1 lb cooked small shelled prawns or shrimps

salt
butter
grated hard cheese to taste
6 oz soft cheese, thinly sliced

First make the Béchamel sauce. Put aside but keep warm.

Cook the lasagne in boiling salted water and drain as described on page 23. Rub a baking dish generously with butter and cover with a layer of lasagne. Add a layer of prawns, spread with sauce, then add a sprinkling of grated cheese and a layer of soft cheese. Repeat this until all the ingredients are finished, the top layer being a mixture of grated and soft cheese. Bake in a moderate oven (350°F., mark 4) for about 30 minutes or until the top is brown, and serve at once.

Fresh, frozen or canned prawns or shrimps can be used in this recipe, also a sprinkling of cooked or frozen, tender green peas.

CHAPTER FOUR

SAVOURY TOP-OF-THE-STOVE

(i) Macaroni

MACARONI WITH BLACK OLIVES AND SALAMI

1 lb macaroni (small thick lengths)
15–20 small black olives, stoned and chopped
2 oz salami, chopped
3 tablespoons (3¾) olive oil
1 onion, finely chopped

1 tablespoon (1¼) tomato paste
¼ pint (⅔ cup) thin cream or top of the milk
3 tablespoons (3¾) grated hard cheese

Cook the macaroni in boiling salted water as described on page 23. Heat the oil in a large pan with 2 tablespoons (2½) of hot water, add the onion and cook until soft. Dilute the tomato paste with ½ cup of hot water. Add to the pan with the olives and salami and stir well. Stir in the cream and cook for a few minutes. Drain the macaroni, return it to the pan or turn into a hot dish, add the sauce and sprinkle with cheese. Serve at once.

MACARONI WITH CAPERS, ANCHOVIES AND BLACK OLIVES

1 lb macaroni (penne or mac-cheroni)
1 tablespoon (1¼) capers
3–4 anchovy fillets
12 black olives, stoned and chopped
¼ cup (⅓) olive oil

1 small chilli pepper
1 clove garlic
2 large ripe tomatoes, peeled and chopped
a little rosemary
black pepper to taste

First prepare the sauce. Heat the oil in a small pan. Add the chilli and garlic and cook until the garlic is brown when it can be discarded. Add the anchovies and cook these until they are dissolved in the oil. They can be squashed with a small wooden spoon in the pan. Add the tomatoes, capers and rosemary, stir well and cook gently for 5 minutes. Discard the chilli.

While the sauce is cooking, cook the macaroni in boiling salted water as described on page 23. Drain, return it to the pan or turn into a warm serving dish, add the sauce, stir and serve at once. Sprinkle each plateful with freshly-ground black pepper.

For this dish, the tomatoes should not be over-cooked, in fact, they should be almost raw.

MACARONI WITH A RICH MEAT SAUCE

1 lb macaroni
1 lb lean meat, cut into cubes
2 oz (4 tablespoons) butter
4–6 strips fat bacon, chopped
1 large onion, chopped
1 stalk celery, chopped
1 carrot, thinly sliced in rounds
2 cups (2½) red wine, beer, dry
   cider or water

1 clove
1 bay leaf
salt and pepper
2 tablespoons (2½) tomato paste
1 cup (1¼) thin cream or top of the
   milk
grated cheese (optional)

Heat the butter and bacon and when the bacon fat runs gently cook the vegetables. Add the meat, raise the heat and, stirring almost all the time, fry until brown. Add the wine, clove, bay leaf, salt and pepper. Cook over a moderate heat until the liquid has been reduced by half. Dilute the tomato paste with ½ cup of hot water, add this to the pan, cover and cook over a low heat until the meat and vegetables are soft. Take out the meat, rub the sauce through a coarse sieve and add the cream. Return to the pan, put back the meat and slowly reheat.

About 10 minutes before taking out the meat, start cooking

the macaroni in boiling salted water as described on page 23. Drain and mix into the meat sauce. Serve immediately with grated cheese separately.

MACARONI WITH A WALNUT SAUCE

1 lb macaroni
½ lb shelled and crushed walnuts
2 tablespoons (2½) each olive oil and water
1 small onion, finely chopped
1 small can peeled tomatoes

salt and pepper
4 tablespoons (5) milk
pinch grated nutmeg
butter
grated hard cheese to taste

First make the sauce. Heat the oil and water, add the onion and cook this gently until soft. Raise the heat, add the tomatoes, crush them well and mix into the onion. Add salt and pepper and cook for 5 minutes. Add the milk, again stir, bring the sauce gently to the boil, add the walnuts and a generous grating of nutmeg. Simmer while the macaroni is cooking.

Cook the macaroni in boiling salted water as described on page 23. Drain and return it to the pan or turn into a hot serving dish. Add the sauce, stir it well into the macaroni and dot with slivers of butter. Serve with grated cheese separately.

MACARONI WITH PAPRIKA SAUCE

1 lb macaroni
2 teaspoons (2½) Hungarian paprika
1½ oz (3 tablespoons) butter
1 small onion, chopped
1 small sweet pepper, cored, seeded and chopped

1 lb ground beef
salt and pepper
1 small can peeled tomatoes, chopped
1 cup (1¼) sour cream or natural unsweetened yoghourt

First prepare the sauce. Heat the butter, add the onion and fry gently until it begins to soften. Add the sweet pepper and cook this for 5 minutes. Add the beef, stir it well to prevent sticking, and cook until it browns. Add salt, pepper, paprika pepper and tomatoes. Stir well and cook for 20 minutes over a moderate heat.

In the meantime cook the macaroni in boiling salted water as described on page 23. Drain, stir it gently but thoroughly into the simmering meat, and cook for 5 minutes. Immediately before serving, add the sour cream. Stir gently and serve.

MACARONI WITH CREAM CHEESE

1 lb macaroni	3 tablespoons ($3\frac{3}{4}$) hot water or
$\frac{1}{2}$ lb cream cheese	stock
salt and pepper	grated cheese to taste
good pinch grated nutmeg	

Cook the macaroni in boiling salted water as described on page 23. While it is cooking make the sauce. Rub the cheese through a sieve, add salt, pepper, nutmeg and hot water, and beat well. Drain the macaroni, then return it to the pan or turn it into a hot dish, add the sauce, mix it well and serve at once with grated cheese.

Instead of water or stock, a dry white wine or dry cider, or even a light beer may be used.

MACARONI WITH GORGONZOLA CHEESE

1 lb macaroni (chifferoni rigati)	3 oz (6 tablespoons) butter
$\frac{1}{4}$ lb gorgonzola	salt and pepper

Cook the macaroni in boiling salted water as described on page 23. While it is cooking, prepare the sauce. Cut the gorgonzola and butter into small pieces and combine with 2 tablespoonfuls of the liquid in which the pasta is cooking. Add pepper, preferably freshly-ground black pepper. Drain the macaroni, return it to the pan or turn into a warm serving dish, add the gorgonzola sauce, mix gently but well and serve at once.

This dish has an unusual and delicate flavour. If preferred, half and half piquant and mild gorgonzola may be used instead of only one kind.

MACARONI WITH A WHITE WINE SAUCE

1 lb macaroni
4 tablespoons (5) olive oil
¼ lb cooked ham, diced
1 clove garlic, chopped
marjoram or parsley, finely chopped, to taste

½ pint (1¼ cups) dry white wine
2 ripe tomatoes, peeled
¼ lb fresh mushrooms, cleaned and sliced
1 cup (1¼) stock or water
grated cheese to taste

First make the sauce. Heat the oil, add the ham, garlic and marjoram, stir well. Cook for 2 minutes, then add the wine. Bring this slowly to the boil, add the tomatoes and mushrooms. Stir well. Add the stock, cover the pan and cook gently.

In the meantime, cook the macaroni in boiling salted water as described on page 23. Drain, return it to the pan or turn into a hot serving dish. Add the sauce, stir well but gently and serve with grated cheese separately.

MACARONI WITH BROWN BEANS

1 lb macaroni (chifferotti rigati)
1 lb cooked or canned brown beans*
3 tablespoons (3¾) olive oil
1 small onion, chopped
2 lb ripe tomatoes, peeled and chopped

¼ lb unsmoked ham, shredded
salt and pepper
1 teaspoon (1¼) sugar
fresh green herbs, chopped
¼ lb grated hard cheese

* If fresh brown beans are used they must be shelled and cooked until almost tender; if canned beans, do not use those that come in a thick sauce. Dried brown beans also may be used but these will require several hours soaking and fairly long cooking.

First make the sauce in a large pan. Heat the oil, put in the onion and, when it is soft, add the tomatoes, ham, salt, pepper and sugar. Bring gently to the boil, then simmer until the sauce is thick. Then add the beans and cook for 10 minutes.

Cook the macaroni in boiling salted water as described on page 23 but for 2 minutes less than the recommended time. Drain the macaroni and at once add it to the sauce, then stir gently with a wooden spoon and cook for 2–3 minutes. Take from the stove, add the chopped herbs and cheese and serve at once.

If possible, make the sauce in a table-to-stove casserole. If unsmoked ham is not available, use very lean bacon.

MACARONI WITH A BRANDY SAUCE

1 lb macaroni (tortiglioni)   coarsely-chopped parsley to taste
½ cup brandy   1 teaspoon (1¼) sugar
2–3 small mild onions   salt to taste
1 lb ripe tomatoes   12 sweet black olives, chopped
¼ cup (⅓) olive oil   coarsely-ground black pepper

First prepare the sauce. Peel and coarsely chop the onions and tomatoes. Heat the oil, add the onions and parsley and simmer until the onions begin to soften but do not let them brown. Add the tomatoes, sugar and salt. Stir and cook over a slow heat until the tomatoes are soft and the sauce is thick and smooth.

Start cooking the macaroni in boiling salted water as described on page 23. While the macaroni is cooking, add the brandy and olives to the sauce. Stir and simmer for 10 minutes. Drain the macaroni and return to the pan or turn into a warm serving dish. Stir the sauce into the macaroni, mix well and serve. Black pepper should be freshly-ground and sprinkled over each plateful.

While it isn't necessary to use the finest brandy to make this sauce it is necessary not to cut down on the amount. Unless the sauce has a strong flavour of brandy there is no point to it.

Although this brandy sauce can be used with most pasta shapes, I have found that it goes best of all with the ribbed pasta shapes. It is perfect with tortiglione, good with denti d'elefante but, for my taste, too strong with the delicate eliche or fusilli rigati.

MACARONI WITH PEAS

1 lb macaroni   1–2 sage leaves or mint
1 lb peas, fresh, frozen or canned   salt
1 oz (2 tablespoons) butter   sugar

Heat the butter, add the sage, cook for a minute or two to get the full flavour into the butter, then add the peas, salt, a little sugar and enough water to just cover the peas. Cook gently until tender.

Cook the macaroni in boiling salted water as described on page 23. Drain, return it to the pan or turn into a hot dish, add the peas with their liquid and serve at once.

If using canned peas, drain them well. If using frozen peas, use the garden type, not petit pois as these will break up in the pasta.

MACARONI AND CANNED MUSHROOM SAUCE

1 lb macaroni   1 onion, finely chopped
1 large can mushrooms   1 small can tomato paste
1 oz (2 tablespoons) butter or   salt and pepper
  other cooking fat   grated cheese to taste

Cook the macaroni in boiling salted water as described on page 23. Heat the butter and fry the onion until soft. Dilute the tomato paste with 1 cup of water, add to the pan with salt and pepper, stir well and cook until the sauce is hot. Drain and chop the mushrooms and add to the pan.

Drain the macaroni, return it to the pan in which it was cooked or turn it into a hot serving dish, add the mushroom sauce, stir and serve with grated cheese separately.

MACARONI WITH BACON AND TOMATOES

1 lb macaroni
2-3 slices smoked bacon, chopped
1 large can tomatoes
½ cup (⅔) olive oil
1-2 cloves garlic, crushed

1 medium-sized onion, finely
  chopped
1 teaspoon (1¼) sugar
salt and pepper
1 cup (1¼) grated cheese

Heat the oil and lightly fry the garlic. Discard the garlic, add the onion and cook until it is transparent. Add the bacon, cook for 2-3 minutes, then add the tomatoes with their liquid, sugar, salt and pepper. Bring gently to the boil, lower the heat and cook for 30 minutes, stirring occasionally.

In the meantime cook the macaroni in boiling salted water as described on page 23. Drain. Put a layer of macaroni into a hot deep serving dish, sprinkle with cheese and 2-3 tablespoonfuls of the sauce, and continue in this manner, working quickly so that the macaroni does not cool, until all the ingredients are finished. Serve immediately.

MACARONI IN 'VELVET SAUCE'

1 lb macaroni (denti d'elefante)
4 tablespoons (5) olive oil
1 large onion, chopped
½ lb (1 cup) diced cooked meat
1 medium-sized can peeled
  tomatoes

salt
½ teaspoon (⅔) sugar
¼ cup (⅓) milk
½ bay leaf
1 oz (2 tablespoons) butter
grated cheese to taste

Heat the oil and gently fry the onion and meat; mash the tomatoes, add to the pan with the salt and sugar, cover and cook gently for 20 minutes. Stir in the milk, add the bay leaf and cook another 2 minutes. Discard the bay leaf and rub the sauce through a sieve.

While the sauce is cooking, cook the macaroni in boiling salted water as described on page 23. Drain, return it to the pan or turn into a warm dish, add the sauce and butter. Serve at once with cheese separately.

MACARONI WITH TOMATO AND EGG SAUCE

1 lb macaroni (tortiglioni)
1 large can peeled tomatoes
2 eggs
3 tablespoons (3¾) olive oil

1 small onion, sliced
salt and pepper to taste
1 clove garlic, crushed
grated cheese to taste

Heat the oil, add the onion and 3 tablespoonfuls of hot water. Cook until the onion is tender. Chop the tomatoes, add to the pan with the salt, pepper and garlic. Raise the heat and cook until the sauce has thickened, about 15 minutes. Discard the garlic. Lightly beat the eggs and add to the sauce, mixing thoroughly.

Cook the macaroni in boiling salted water as described on page 23. Drain and return it to the pan or turn into a hot dish. Add the sauce and stir gently but thoroughly. Serve at once with cheese separately.

MACARONI WITH BUTTER AND SAGE

1 lb macaroni (fusilli rigati)
4 oz (½ cup) butter

4 sage leaves

Cook the macaroni in boiling salted water as described on page 23. Gently heat the butter in a large pan, preferably one which can be brought to the table, add the sage, and when the butter begins to brown, discard the sage. Drain the macaroni, turn it into the hot butter, mix gently and serve at once.

(ii) Noodles

NOODLES WITH COURGETTE SAUCE

1 lb noodles (tagliatelle mezzane) *2 tablespoons ($2\frac{1}{2}$) olive oil*
$\frac{1}{2}$ lb small courgettes (zucchini), *1 small onion, minced*
 thinly sliced   *salt and pepper to taste*
1 oz (2 tablespoons) butter *grated cheese*

Heat half the butter with all the oil in a small pan, add the onion, the courgettes and $\frac{1}{2}$ cupful of hot water. Cook over a low heat, stirring often until the liquid has evaporated. Season.

 Cook the noodles in boiling salted water as described on page 23. Drain, return to the pan or turn them into a hot dish. Add the courgette sauce, the remaining butter, and the cheese. Stir well but gently and serve at once.

NOODLES WITH A PARSLEY AND WALNUT SAUCE

1 lb noodles (linguine) *1 small clove garlic (optional)*
3–4 sprigs parsley   *3 tablespoons ($3\frac{3}{4}$) olive oil*
$\frac{1}{4}$ lb shelled walnuts   *3 tablespoons ($3\frac{3}{4}$) grated cheese*
$\frac{1}{2}$ teaspoon ($\frac{2}{3}$) dried marjoram or *salt to taste*
 oregano

Cook the noodles in boiling salted water as described on page 23. Mix the remaining ingredients in a blender, adding 2–3 tablespoonfuls of the noodle liquid. Drain the noodles, return to the pan or turn them into a hot dish, and pour the sauce over the top. Serve at once.

'STRAW AND HAY' NOODLES WITH A CHICKEN LIVER SAUCE (1)

½ lb each yellow and green noodles (fettuccine)
½ lb chicken livers, chopped
2 tablespoons (2½) olive oil
6 anchovy fillets
1 clove garlic, crushed
1 small onion, minced

1 tablespoon (1¼) capers
1–2 sprigs parsley, chopped
juice ½ lemon
¼ lb fat bacon, chopped
1 cup (1¼) red wine
pepper

Chop the chicken livers and put aside. Heat the oil and cook the anchovy fillets in it until they are dissolved. Add the garlic, let this brown, then discard it. Now add the onion, capers, parsley, lemon juice and bacon and, as the fat of the bacon begins to run, put in the chicken livers. Let these just change colour, then add the wine. Cook over a good heat for 5 minutes, then give a generous sprinkling of freshly-grated pepper.

While the sauce is cooking, cook the noodles in boiling salted water as described on page 23. Drain and return to the pan or turn into a hot serving dish, pour the chicken liver sauce over the top, stir gently and serve at once.

If the sauce is ready before the pasta, this can be kept simmering for a short time without spoiling; but if the pasta is ready first and has to wait for the sauce, it will spoil. Some fettuccine take longer to cook than others, so follow the instructions on the packet carefully.

'STRAW AND HAY' NOODLES WITH A CREAM SAUCE (2)

½ lb each green and yellow noodles (fettuccine)
3 oz (6 tablespoons) butter

1 teaspoon (1¼) plain flour
1 cup (1¼) single cream
4 tablespoons (5) grated cheese

Cook the noodles in boiling salted water as described on page 23. Drain.

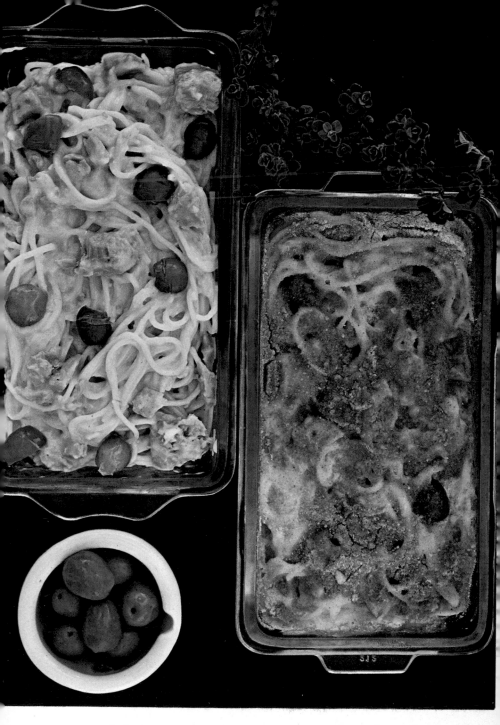

3. Baked Macaroni and Canned Salmon Custard
(before and after baking)

4. Macaroni with Black Olives and Salami

5. 'Straw and Hay' or Noodles with a Cream Sauce

6. Noodles with Pesto

While the noodles are cooking, make the sauce. Heat half the butter, add the flour and stir until smooth. Add the cream and stir over a low heat for 3 minutes. Pour this sauce over the drained noodles, add the remaining butter and cheese, preferably Parmesan, and serve at once.

'STRAW AND HAY' NOODLES WITH A TOMATO SAUCE (3)

½ lb each green and yellow noodles (fettuccine)
3–4 canned peeled tomatoes, sieved
1 oz (2 tablespoons) butter

2 teaspoons (2½) plain flour
½ cup (⅔) single cream
salt and pepper

First make the sauce. Heat the butter, add the flour and stir until smooth. Take from the heat, add the tomatoes, stir well, then return to the stove and cook gently for 10 minutes, stirring all the time. Add the cream, salt and pepper and stir well. Cover, put aside but keep hot.

Cook the noodles in boiling salted water as described on page 23, starting after the sauce has been cooking for 5 minutes. Drain and return to the pan or turn into a hot serving dish. Immediately add the sauce, stir well but gently and serve.

NOODLES WITH PESTO

1 lb noodles (trenette)
4 oz (about ¾ cup) pesto (see page 137)

2 medium-sized potatoes, slightly less than ½ lb
3 oz (1 cup) grated cheese

Peel the potatoes and cut them into thin strips. Have ready a large pan with plenty of boiling salted water, at least 12 pints (15). Add the potatoes. Cook for 2 minutes, then add the noodles and cook as described on page 23. Take 2–3 tablespoonfuls of the liquid in which the noodles are cooking and dilute the *pesto*. Keep this hot. Drain and turn the noodles into a hot serving dish

3

or back into the hot pan. Add the *pesto* and mix it well into the noodles. Serve at once with a bowl of grated cheese separately.

NOODLES WITH MEAT AND VEGETABLES

1 lb noodles (trenette)
¼ lb ground meat
¼ lb fat bacon
1 stalk celery
1 each large onion, carrot
1–2 sweet peppers

4 tablespoons (5) olive oil
1 lb runner beans
1 lb ripe tomatoes or equivalent if canned
salt and pepper to taste

Cut the bacon, celery, onion, carrot and sweet peppers into small pieces. Heat the oil in a large casserole, add the bacon, cook until its fat runs, then add the meat and stir well to prevent lumps forming. Fry until it changes colour. Trim the beans and break into chunky pieces and add to the pan. While these are cooking, scald the tomatoes, peel and chop. Add to the pan with salt and pepper. Cover the pan and cook gently for 1 hour. Stir from time to time.

Towards the end of cooking time for the sauce, cook the noodles in boiling salted water as described on page 23. Drain and combine with the cooked vegetables and serve at once.

NOODLES WITH CHICKEN

1 lb noodles (tagliarelli)
6 pieces chicken
salt and pepper
3 oz (6 tablespoons) butter or other fat
2 onions, finely chopped
1 clove garlic, pounded

hot water
6 peeled tomatoes, chopped
½ pint (⅔) thick tomato soup
3 stalks celery, chopped
1 large sprig parsley, chopped
¼ teaspoon (⅓) ground cinnamon
grated cheese

Rub the chicken pieces with salt and pepper. Heat the butter in a large pan. Add the chicken pieces and cook until brown all over.

Take from the pan, put aside but keep hot. Add the onions and garlic and fry them until they begin to change colour. Return the chicken to the pan, add 1 cupful of hot water (if you use either white wine or beer, all the better) and cook for 15 minutes over a low heat. Add the tomatoes, tomato soup, celery, parsley, salt, pepper and enough hot water to just cover. Continue cooking over a moderate heat until the chicken is tender.

When the chicken pieces are tender, cook the noodles in boiling salted water as described on page 23. Drain.

At this point add the cinnamon to the pan with the chicken and stir it well into the sauce. Take the chicken pieces from the pan. Turn the noodles into a hot serving dish or platter, add the sauce and grated cheese, stirring these well into the noodles. Arrange the chicken pieces either on top of the noodles or round the sides of the platter. Serve at once.

NOODLES WITH GARLIC, PARSLEY AND OIL SAUCE

1 lb noodles (linguine)
2–3 cloves garlic, finely chopped

3 large sprigs parsley, finely chopped
½ pint (1¼ cups) olive oil

Cook the noodles in boiling salted water as described on page 23. Heat the oil, add the garlic and fry until it is brown. Remove and discard. Add the parsley and continue to cook for a few minutes. Drain the noodles, return to the pan or turn into a hot dish, add the oil with the parsley, stir well and serve.

NOODLES WITH BRANDY RAISIN SAUCE

1 lb narrow noodles (tagliatelle)
4 tablespoons (5) brandy
3 tablespoons (3¾) seedless raisins
1 oz (2 tablespoons) butter
1 large, hard apple, diced

½ pint (1¼ cups) thin cream or top of the milk
2 egg yolks, beaten
salt and pepper to taste

Soak the raisins in the brandy. Cook the noodles in boiling salted water as described on page 23. Heat half the butter, add the apple and gently fry until golden brown; add the raisins and brandy, cream, egg yolks, salt and pepper. Stir gently and cook for 1 minute. Quickly drain the noodles, return to the hot pan or turn into a hot dish, add the sauce, the remaining butter and stir well. Serve at once.

NOODLES WITH CREAM CHEESE (1)

1 lb flat noodles (tagliatelle)
½ lb cream cheese
3–4 strips fat bacon

1 cup (1¼) sour cream or natural
yoghourt
fresh or dried dill, chopped, to taste

Cook the noodles in boiling salted water as described on page 23. While they are cooking, chop the bacon and fry in a wide pan over a low heat until crisp. Take out the bacon and put aside. As soon as the noodles are cooked, drain them and turn into the pan in which the bacon was cooked, stir well, lower the heat and add the sour cream. Again stir, then take from the heat, add the cheese and dill and sprinkle the fried bacon over the top. Serve at once.

NOODLES WITH CREAM CHEESE (2)

1 lb noodles (tagliatelle)
6 oz (¾ cup) cream cheese

4 oz (½ cup) butter
paprika pepper

Cook the noodles in boiling salted water as described on page 23. Drain and return to the pan or turn into a hot fire-proof dish. Add the butter, stir it well until melted; add the cheese and gently cook until the noodles are completely covered with butter and cheese – do not let the noodles boil or they will become too soft. Serve at once, sprinkled with paprika pepper.

NOODLES WITH FENNEL

There are several varieties of fennel, a vegetable which has a strong aniseed flavour and is exceedingly popular in the South of Italy. It is also becoming increasingly popular in other countries. In this recipe it is the large bulb fennel which is called for. One pound of fennel is roughly two or three bulbs, depending on their size.

1 lb noodles (tagliatelle mezzane)   *grated hard cheese, preferably*
1 lb bulb fennel   *Parmesan*
olive oil

Thoroughly wash the fennel, cut the bulbs into halves, then cook in salted water to cover until tender. Drain, reserving the liquid. Gently squeeze the fennel dry and thinly slice into strips. Put aside but keep hot.

Bring a pan with plenty of salted water, plus the fennel liquid, to the boil, add the noodles and cook as described on page 23 until *al dente*. Drain quickly, return to the hot pan, add the fennel, stir gently and serve at once.

Serve sprinkled lightly with olive oil and with plenty of grated cheese.

NOODLES WITH WHITE CABBAGE

1 lb noodles (tagliatelle mezzane)   *1 small chopped onion*
1 small white cabbage   *salt and pepper*
3 oz (6 tablespoons) cooking fat or
*   butter*

Shred the cabbage. Heat the fat in a pan, add the cabbage and onion and fry for 5 minutes. Add just enough water to cover the bottom of the pan, cover and cook until the cabbage is tender.

Cook the noodles in boiling salted water as described on

page 23. Drain and return to the pan in which they were cooked or turn into a hot serving dish. Mix the cabbage, onion and fat into the noodles, sprinkle with pepper and serve at once.

Fried diced bacon, croûtons, capers or paprika pepper can be added to the cabbage, if liked.

NOODLES WITH CHICKEN LIVER SAUCE

1 lb noodles (tagliatelle)
½ lb chicken livers, chopped
2 tablespoons (2½) olive oil
1 small onion, minced

2 sage leaves
2 teaspoons (2½) plain flour
2 tablespoons (2½) dry sherry
salt and pepper to taste

Heat the oil, add the onion, sage and 2 tablespoonfuls of water. When the onion is tender, add the chicken livers and fry for a few minutes. Sprinkle with flour and add the sherry and seasoning. Stir gently and cook for 5 minutes over a very low heat.

While the sauce is cooking, cook the noodles in boiling salted water as described on page 23. Quickly drain, return to the pan or turn into a hot dish, add the sauce, stir and serve at once.

NOODLES WITH ARTICHOKES

1 lb noodles (lasagnette)
6–8 small canned artichokes or
  6 artichoke hearts
3 tablespoons (3¾) olive oil
1 onion, minced
1 tablespoon (1¼) minced parsley

salt and pepper
½ cup (⅔) grated hard cheese,
  preferably Parmesan
2 oz (4 tablespoons) butter
  (optional)

Heat the oil with the same quantity of water. Add the onion, cook for 3 minutes, then add the parsley, artichokes, salt and pepper. Cover the pan and cook gently to heat the artichokes. Take the pan from the heat, add the cheese, stir gently but well and return to the stove. Simmer for a few minutes.

While the sauce is cooking, cook the noodles in boiling salted water as described on page 23. Drain, return to the pan or turn into a hot serving dish, add the sauce and gently stir. Garnish with slivers of butter, if liked.

NOODLES AND PÂTÉ

1 lb narrow green noodles (fettuc-   *4 oz (½ cup) butter*
cine)   *½ lb pâté (soft paste variety)*

Cook the noodles in boiling salted water as described on page 23. Drain and turn at once into the dish in which they are to be served. While the noodles are cooking, cut the butter and pâté into small pieces. Mix these at once into the hot noodles. Serve immediately, before the pâté has melted.

NOODLES WITH BUTTER AND PARMESAN CHEESE

1 lb noodles (fettuccine)   *2 cups (2½) grated Parmesan cheese*
4 oz (½ cup) butter   *salt and pepper*

Cook the noodles in boiling salted water as described on page 23. Drain and turn into a hot serving dish and mix in the butter, stirring it well into the noodles; add the cheese, stir again, sprinkle with salt and pepper, and serve at once. Be generous with the butter. Spaghetti can be prepared in the same way.

NOODLES WITH A PIQUANT SAUCE

1 lb narrow noodles   *4–5 anchovy fillets, chopped*
2–3 tablespoons oil   *½ lb tomatoes, peeled and chopped*
1–2 cloves garlic, finely chopped   *coarsely-chopped parsley to taste*
finely-chopped red chilli to taste   *salt and pepper (optional)*

Cook the noodles in boiling salted water as described on page 23. While the water is boiling and the noodles are cooking, prepare the sauce. Heat the oil, add the garlic and the chopped chilli and cook until the garlic just begins to change colour. Add the anchovies, cook these until they are dissolved in the oil, then add the tomatoes, stir the mixture well and continue cooking over a low heat until the sauce is thick. Just before serving add the parsley.

Drain the noodles, turn into a hot dish, add the sauce and serve immediately.

This sauce does not require the addition of salt and pepper as the anchovies are quite salty but test for seasoning before serving. Whether you add pepper will depend on the quantity of chilli used.

(iii) Spaghetti

SPAGHETTI RUSTIC STYLE

1 lb spaghetti (bucatini)	½ oz (2 tablespoons) flour
1 oz (2 tablespoons) butter	¼ pint (⅔ cup) red wine
1 tablespoon (1¼) oil	salt and pepper
1–2 onions, finely chopped	pinch thyme
4 oz continental-type sausage	grated cheese

Cook the spaghetti in plenty of boiling salted water as described on page 23. Heat the butter and oil in a small pan, add the onion(s) and fry until they begin to change colour. Add the sausage meat and mix it all very thoroughly. Sprinkle with flour, stir, add the wine and again stir well. Add enough hot water to make a thick but slightly fluid sauce. Add salt, pepper and thyme, all to taste. Leave to simmer until required.

Drain the spaghetti and turn out on to a hot dish. Add the sauce and generously top with grated cheese. Serve at once.

Only a coarse smoked pork sausage should be used with this recipe. If this is not available, diced cooked meat would be a suitable substitute.

SPAGHETTI WITH CHEESE AND PEPPER

1 lb spaghetti (pasta gemma, see   grated Parmesan cheese to taste
  p. 30)   freshly-ground black pepper

Cook the spaghetti in boiling salted water as described on page
23. Drain but not too well for a light film of water should
remain on the spaghetti. Serve very hot with grated cheese and
freshly-milled black pepper.

A dish for those with a real appreciation of the flavour of good
spaghetti.

SPAGHETTI WITH CREAM CHEESE (1)

1 lb spaghetti   salt and pepper
¾ lb (1 cup) cream cheese   2½ oz (5 tablespoons) butter
3 oz (1 cup) grated hard cheese

Cook the spaghetti in boiling salted water as described on
page 23. Beat the cream cheese with a wooden spoon until light
and fluffy or rub it through a sieve. Mix it with the grated cheese,
add salt and pepper. Just melt the butter. As soon as the spaghetti
is cooked, drain it quickly and return it to the pan or turn into a
hot dish, add the melted butter, stir rapidly, then stir in the cheese
mixture. Mix this swiftly into the spaghetti and serve at once.

SPAGHETTI WITH CREAM CHEESE (2)

1 lb spaghetti   black pepper
½ lb cream cheese   4–6 tablespoons (5–7½) grated hard
½ cup (⅔) cream or milk   cheese
2 oz (4 tablespoons) butter,
  creamed

Cook the spaghetti in boiling salted water as described on
page 23. While it is cooking, prepare the sauce. Beat the cream

cheese in a deep serving dish, add the cream, butter and pepper. Mix thoroughly and put aside. Now drain the spaghetti, turn it at once into the serving dish, mix well and serve with grated cheese separately.

SPAGHETTI WITH A TOMATO AND BACON SAUCE

1 lb spaghetti
1 lb ripe tomatoes, peeled and chopped
¼ lb bacon, diced
2 tablespoons (2½) olive oil
1 onion, thinly sliced
sprig oregano or marjoram or parsley
1 cup (1¼) grated hard cheese

If ripe tomatoes are not available, use canned tomatoes, drained.

Heat the oil, add the bacon and fry until the fat has been rendered; add the onion, stir well and cook until soft but not brown. Add the tomatoes to the pan with the oregano, bring to the boil, reduce the heat and cook for 25–30 minutes. Remove the oregano before serving the sauce.

While the sauce is cooking, cook the spaghetti in boiling salted water as described on page 23. Drain and turn into a hot serving dish or back into the hot pan. Add the sauce, stir it quickly into the spaghetti and serve at once, with grated cheese.

SPAGHETTI WITH A TOMATO AND MEATBALL SAUCE

1 lb spaghetti
4 oz (¾ cup) tomato paste
½ lb ground cooked meat
½ lb sausage meat, crumbled
1 thick slice white bread
4 tablespoons (5) grated hard cheese
1 tablespoon (1¼) minced parsley
1 clove garlic, minced
1–2 eggs, well beaten
1 small onion, minced
4 tablespoons (5) olive oil
nutmeg
salt and pepper to taste

Dilute the tomato paste with 2 cupfuls of warm water.

Soak the bread in water until soft and squeeze quite dry. Combine the bread, meat, sausage meat, cheese, parsley, garlic, eggs and onion with 1 tablespoon (1¼) of oil and a good grating of nutmeg, salt and pepper. Knead the mixture well. Break off small pieces and shape these into walnut-sized balls. If the mixture should feel too loose (and much depends on the size of the eggs), add just enough flour to make it firm.

Heat the remaining oil and fry the meat balls gently until brown. Add the diluted tomato paste.

While the meatballs are cooking, cook the spaghetti in boiling salted water as described on page 23. Drain, turn into a hot serving dish, add the meatballs and their sauce and serve at once. It is better not to stir the meatballs into the spaghetti but drop them on top.

SPAGHETTI WITH UNCOOKED TOMATO AND CHEESE SAUCE

1 lb spaghetti
3–4 ripe tomatoes, peeled and chopped
¼ lb diced soft cheese

3 tablespoons (3¾) grated cheese
1 clove garlic
salt and pepper to taste
mixed herbs, chopped

Cook the spaghetti in boiling salted water as described on page 23. While it is cooking, prepare the sauce. Rub a deep serving dish with the garlic. If a strong garlic flavour is preferred, the garlic can be finely chopped and mixed in with the other ingredients. Add the tomatoes, cheeses, salt, pepper and herbs. Stir well.

By this time the spaghetti will be cooked. Drain it quickly and at once stir into the sauce. Mix well and serve at once.

SPAGHETTI WITH TOMATOES AND BLACK OLIVES

1 lb spaghetti
1 small can peeled tomatoes
12 small black olives, stoned and chopped
3 tablespoons (3¾) each olive oil and water

1 small onion, finely sliced
½ teaspoon (⅔) dried oregano or marjoram
1 clove garlic, chopped
pepper to taste
2 tablespoons (2½) milk

Heat the oil with the water, add the onion and cook until soft. Add the tomatoes, crush them and bring to a rapid boil. Cook for 10 minutes or until the sauce has thickened; add the olives, oregano, garlic, pepper and milk. Cook for another 10 minutes.

While the sauce is cooking, cook the spaghetti in boiling salted water as described on page 23. Return it to the pan or turn into a hot dish, add the sauce and stir well. Serve at once.

SPAGHETTI WITH A BACON SAUCE

1 lb spaghetti
¼ lb bacon
1 small sweet red pepper
1 lb tomatoes, peeled and chopped
2 tablespoons (2½) lard or olive oil

1 small onion, finely chopped
1 clove garlic
salt and black pepper
1 cup (1¼) grated hard cheese

Dice the sweet pepper, discarding the core and seeds. Chop the bacon. Heat the fat and fry the bacon until it is crisp and brown, take from the pan but keep it hot. Add the onion, garlic and sweet pepper to the pan and fry them gently until the onion begins to brown. Discard the garlic and stir in the tomatoes. Add salt and plenty of pepper. Cook for 30 minutes. Return the bacon to the pan.

When the sauce has been cooking for about 20 minutes, cook the spaghetti in boiling salted water as described on page 23. Drain and turn into a hot serving dish or back into the hot pan. Stir the sauce into the spaghetti and sprinkle with cheese.

SPAGHETTI WITH BACON AND EGG SAUCE

1 lb spaghetti
6 thin strips bacon, diced
4 eggs
2 tablespoons (2½) olive oil

½ cup (⅔) milk
1 cup (1¼) grated hard cheese
salt and black pepper

Cook the spaghetti in boiling salted water as described on page 23. Heat the oil in a shallow casserole, add the bacon and fry it until crisp. Add the milk, lower the heat and cook for a few minutes. Beat the eggs in a bowl, add the grated cheese and continue to beat until blended. Season. Heat the plates on which the spaghetti is to be served. When the spaghetti is ready, quickly drain it and put into the pan with the bacon and stir rapidly. Add the egg and cheese mixture and stir it quickly into the spaghetti. The eggs should, and will, cook immediately if the spaghetti is sufficiently hot. Whatever happens, the spaghetti must not be allowed to cool after the egg mixture has been added. Stir for a minute or so, no longer, and serve at once on the hot plates.

Instead of milk, a dry white wine or cider can be used.

SPAGHETTI WITH BACON, HAM
AND CROÛTONS

1 lb spaghetti
1 thick slice fat bacon – about ¼ lb
1 thick slice lean ham – about ¼ lb

2 oz (3 cups) diced stale bread
2 oz (4 tablespoons) butter

Cook the spaghetti in boiling salted water as described on page 23. While it is cooking, prepare the remaining ingredients.

Cut the bacon and ham into dice about the same size as the diced bread. Heat the butter, add the bacon, let this cook a little until the fat begins to run, then add the ham, mix well, and finally add the diced bread, stirring all the time and fry this until it is brown.

Drain the spaghetti and return it to the saucepan. Add the fried ingredients, stirring them well into the spaghetti. Serve at once.

SPAGHETTI RIVIERA STYLE

1 lb spaghetti
1 large sweet pepper
4 tablespoons (5) olive oil
1½ oz (3 tablespoons) butter
1 large onion, thinly sliced
1-2 cloves garlic, minced

2 tablespoons (2½) minced parsley
4 oz (¾ cup) tomato paste
salt and pepper
1 teaspoon (1¼) sugar
12 black olives, stoned
grated hard cheese (optional)

Cut the sweet pepper into thin strips, discarding the core and seeds. Heat the oil together with the butter, add the onion and sweet pepper and cook until the onion is soft. Add the garlic and parsley and continue cooking for 5 minutes. Dilute the tomato paste with 1 cupful of water, add to the pan with the salt, pepper and sugar and cook for about 20 minutes. Add the olives and continue cooking for 5 minutes.

While the sauce is cooking, cook the spaghetti in boiling salted water as described on page 23. Drain, return it to the hot saucepan or turn into a hot dish, add the tomato sauce, stir gently and serve the grated cheese separately, if using.

SPAGHETTI BOLOGNA STYLE

1 lb spaghetti
2 cups (2½) hot Bolognese sauce
(see page 129)

a few slivers butter
2 cups (2½) Parmesan cheese

First make the sauce and keep it simmering until the spaghetti is ready.

Cook the spaghetti in boiling salted water as described on

page 23. Drain and turn into a hot serving dish or back into the pan. Sprinkle with slivers of butter, add half the cheese and half the sauce and quickly mix. Serve the rest of the cheese and sauce separately.

Although Parmesan cheese is traditionally used in Bologna, other hard cheese may be substituted.

SPAGHETTI WITH EGGS AND SAUSAGE MEAT

1 lb spaghetti	*4 tablespoons (5) olive oil*
3–4 eggs	*4 tablespoons (5) milk*
½ lb sausage meat, preferably pork	*grated cheese to taste*

Heat the oil, add the sausage meat, separating it well with a fork. Cook gently until it is brown. Lightly beat the eggs with the milk.

While the sauce is cooking, cook the spaghetti in boiling salted water as described on page 23. Just before draining, add the egg mixture to the sausage meat, stirring until the eggs are set. Leave it over the lowest possible heat.

Drain the spaghetti quickly, return it to the pan or turn into a hot serving dish, add the egg and sausage mixture, stir well, and serve at once, with grated cheese separately.

SPAGHETTI WITH LAMB CUTLETS

½ lb spaghetti	*a large onion, chopped*
12 lamb cutlets	*1 clove garlic, chopped*
4 tomatoes, peeled and chopped	*salt and pepper*
1–2 tablespoons (1¼–2½) tomato paste	*2 pints (2½) water*

Put the cutlets into a large shallow saucepan. Add the tomatoes, the paste, diluted with a little water, the onion, garlic, salt, pepper and half the water. Cook slowly until the meat is tender. Add the remaining water and bring to the boil.

Break the spaghetti into small pieces. Add to the pan and cook until tender, about 15 minutes. Stir the spaghetti into the sauce to distribute it evenly, and serve hot.

SPAGHETTI WITH PORK SAUSAGE AND WHITE WINE SAUCE

1 lb spaghetti (spaghettini)
½ lb Italian pork sausage (see below)
½ cup (⅔) dry white wine

1 sage leaf
a little rosemary
1 bay leaf
2 egg yolks

Skin and crumble the sausages and gently fry the sausage meat in a large pan without adding any fat. Add herbs. When the meat is brown, remove the herbs and add the wine.

While the sausages are cooking, cook the spaghetti in boiling salted water as described on page 23. Drain and stir it into the sausage meat. Beat the egg yolks with 2 tablespoonfuls of the spaghetti liquid. Quickly stir this into the spaghetti and serve at once.

Pork sausages, Italian style, are usually available in Continental delicatessen stores. They are made with meat and fat only. When not available, use coarsely-ground fresh pork with some of its fat.

SPAGHETTI WITH A CHAMPAGNE AND BUTTER SAUCE

1 lb spaghetti (pasta gemma, see p. 30)
½ bottle champagne
2 oz (4 tablespoons) butter
4 thin strips bacon, diced

3 egg yolks
¼ teaspoon (⅓) dry mustard
2 oz (1 cup) diced Gruyère cheese
1 cup (1¼) grated Parmesan cheese

Cook the spaghetti in boiling salted water as described on page 23.

Meanwhile melt the butter in a fairly large pan, add the bacon and gently fry for 2–3 minutes. Add the champagne, stir, cover the pan and simmer for 5 minutes. Beat the egg yolks in a bowl with the mustard and cheeses.

Drain the spaghetti quickly and stir it at once into the pan with the champagne and bacon. Stir quickly but gently, take from the heat, add the egg and cheese mixture, and serve at once.

SPAGHETTI WITH A RED WINE SAUCE

1 lb spaghetti
1 cup (1¼) red wine
¼ cup (⅓) olive oil
2 onions, finely chopped
½ lb ground meat
mixed green herbs to taste
1 bay leaf
1 clove garlic, finely chopped

1 green pepper, cored, seeded and diced
2–3 courgettes (zucchini), thinly sliced
1 lb peeled and chopped tomatoes
salt and pepper to taste
1 teaspoon (1¼) sugar

Heat the oil, add the onions and cook these gently until quite soft but without browning. Add the meat, cook this slowly until it changes colour. Add the herbs, garlic, all the vegetables, salt, pepper and sugar. Stir well, add the wine, cover and cook until the sauce is thick and soft. Allow about 1 hour for cooking the sauce.

About 10–12 minutes before the sauce is ready, cook the spaghetti in boiling salted water as described on page 23. Drain and return it to the pan or turn into a hot dish, add the sauce and stir it well into the spaghetti.

SPAGHETTI WITH CAPERS AND BLACK OLIVES

1 lb long spaghetti
1 tablespoon (1¼) capers
12 black olives, pitted and coarsely chopped
1 cup (1¼) olive oil

1 clove garlic, crushed (optional)
4–6 anchovy fillets, chopped
2–3 good sprigs parsley, finely chopped

Cook the spaghetti in boiling salted water as described on page 23. While it is cooking, make the sauce. Heat the oil, add the garlic (if using), and when this is brown take from the pan and discard. Add the anchovies, stir and cook until these are dissolved in the oil. Add the parsley, stir well, add the capers and olives, stir and cook for 1 minute.

Drain the spaghetti, put into a hot dish or back into the pan, add the sauce, mix well and serve.

For those who like tomatoes, add 2–3 peeled and chopped tomatoes to the pan, cooking them in the oil until soft after the anchovies have dissolved.

SPAGHETTI WITH PARSLEY

1 lb spaghetti
6–7 sprigs parsley, chopped

½ clove garlic, crushed
2 oz (4 tablespoons) butter

Cook the spaghetti in boiling salted water as described on page 23. Rub the garlic round the inside of a casserole. Melt the butter in the casserole, add the parsley and stir. Put aside but keep hot. Drain the spaghetti, add to the casserole, stir and serve at once in the casserole.

SPAGHETTI WITH BUTTER AND
PARMESAN CHEESE

1 lb spaghetti
3 oz (6 tablespoons) butter

grated Parmesan cheese to taste

Cook the spaghetti in boiling salted water as described on page 23. Drain and return it to the pan or turn into a hot dish, add the butter and sprinkle with Parmesan cheese. Serve at once.

SPAGHETTI WITH GARLIC AND OIL

1 lb spaghetti
2–3 cloves garlic, slivered
½ cup (⅔) olive oil

1 small sweet pepper
1 sprig parsley, finely chopped

Finely chop the sweet pepper, discarding the core and seeds.
Cook the spaghetti in boiling salted water as described on page
23. Heat the oil and brown the garlic. Add the parsley and sweet
pepper and gently fry until brown. Drain the spaghetti and return
it to the pan or turn into a hot serving dish, add the sauce, toss
well but lightly and serve at once.

SPAGHETTI WITH GARLIC AND PEPPER SAUCE

1 lb spaghetti
4 cloves garlic, finely chopped
½ teaspoon (⅔) cayenne pepper

1 cup (1¼) olive oil
3–4 sprigs parsley, finely chopped
freshly-ground black pepper

Cook the spaghetti in boiling salted water as described on
page 23. While it is cooking, prepare the sauce. Heat the oil,
add the garlic, cayenne pepper and parsley. Cook slowly – if the
garlic burns it becomes bitter.

Drain the spaghetti, turn it into the pan in which it was cooked
or into a hot serving dish, add the sauce, sprinkle generously with
black pepper, and serve.

SPAGHETTI WITH BÉCHAMEL SAUCE

1 lb spaghetti
1 pint (1¼) Béchamel sauce (see
    page 138)
¼ lb grated hard cheese

6 hard-boiled eggs
peeled tomatoes, sliced
coarsely-chopped parsley

First make the sauce. Add the cheese, cook the sauce until the cheese has melted, cover and put aside but keep hot.

Cook the spaghetti in boiling salted water as described on page 23.

Cut the eggs into halves lengthwise. Drain and arrange the spaghetti in a mound on a large hot platter and border it with the hard-boiled eggs and tomatoes. Garnish with parsley. Serve with the hot cheese sauce.

SPAGHETTI WITH WHITE WINE SAUCE

1 lb spaghetti
1 cup (1¼) dry white wine
3 tablespoons (3¾) olive oil
1 oz (2 tablespoons) butter
1 tablespoon (1¼) plain flour
2 tablespoons (2½) milk

1½ tablespoons (scant 2) pine nuts, chopped
1 tablespoon (1¼) minced parsley
1 clove garlic, minced
salt and pepper to taste

Cook the spaghetti in boiling salted water as described on page 23. Heat the oil and butter in a pan. Mix the flour to a paste with the milk. Add to the pan, stirring gently. Cook for 3 minutes. Add the remaining ingredients and cook another 2 minutes. Drain the spaghetti, return it to the pan or turn it into a hot dish, add the sauce and stir gently. Serve immediately.

SPAGHETTI WITH YOGHOURT

1 lb spaghetti
1 pint (1¼) natural yoghourt, unsweetened

¼ lb (1 cup) butter
1 clove garlic, crushed
paprika pepper to taste

Cook the spaghetti in boiling salted water as described on page 23. Drain and keep in the colander. Quickly melt the butter in the spaghetti pan, add the garlic and cook for 1 minute. Discard the garlic. Return the spaghetti to the pan and stir it well into the hot butter. Add the yoghourt, stir it into the spaghetti and gently heat. Serve at once, sprinkled with paprika pepper.

SPAGHETTI WITH EGG AND CREAM SAUCE

1 lb spaghetti (fidelini)
2 egg yolks
¼ pint (⅔ cup) cream
4 tablespoons (5) grated cheese

2 oz (4 tablespoons) butter,
  softened
salt and pepper to taste

Cook the spaghetti very carefully – it can easily over-cook – in boiling salted water as described on page 23. While it is cooking, combine the remaining ingredients and beat well. Drain the spaghetti, return it to the pan or into a hot dish, add the sauce and serve at once.

SPAGHETTI WITH A TOMATO SAUCE

1 lb spaghetti
1 lb ripe tomatoes
2 tablespoons (2½) olive oil
1 onion, finely chopped
1 stalk celery, finely chopped

1 carrot, finely chopped
salt and pepper
a few leaves basil or other fresh
  herb
grated cheese

Peel and chop the tomatoes. Heat the oil in a pan, add the onion and fry until it browns. Add the tomatoes, celery, carrot, salt and pepper. Cover and cook for about 30 minutes. Add the basil and continue cooking for another 10 minutes. Remove the basil from the sauce and rub the tomatoes and onion through a sieve. While the sauce is cooking, cook the spaghetti in boiling salted water as described on page 23. Drain the spaghetti, turn into a warm dish and pour the sauce over the top. Immediately before serving, stir the sauce into the spaghetti. Serve with cheese.

SPAGHETTI WITH ANCHOVIES AND BUTTERED BREADCRUMBS

1 lb spaghetti
1 oz (2 tablespoons) butter
2 oz (1 cup) soft white breadcrumbs

2 tablespoons (2½) olive oil
2 cloves garlic, finely chopped
5–6 anchovy fillets, chopped
 parsley, coarsely chopped

Cook the spaghetti in boiling salted water as described on page 23. Heat the butter, add the breadcrumbs and fry quickly, stirring all the time until brown. Turn into a bowl. Add the oil to the pan and fry the garlic and anchovies.

Drain the spaghetti, turn on to a hot dish, add the buttered breadcrumbs and stir them well into the spaghetti. Add the garlic and anchovies, again stir and serve at once, sprinkled with coarsely-chopped parsley.

SPAGHETTI WITH AN UNCOOKED TOMATO SAUCE

1 lb spaghetti
1 lb very ripe red tomatoes
1 clove garlic

2 tablespoons (2½) olive oil
chopped green herbs to taste
salt and pepper

Cook the spaghetti in boiling salted water as described on page 23. Scald the tomatoes in boiling water, peel and chop. Finely chop the garlic. Mix with the olive oil and the remaining ingredients in a jar or cocktail shaker and shake until the tomatoes are pulpy and the mixture is shaken to a thick sauce.

When the spaghetti is cooked and drained, pour the uncooked sauce over it and serve at once. No cheese is required.

(iv) Small Shapes

MACARONI WITH A PINE NUT SAUCE

1 lb macaroni (mezze maniche)
½ cup (⅔) pine nuts
3 tablespoons (3¾) olive oil
1 small piece chilli

2 tablespoons (2½) brandy or dry
  white wine
a little coarsely-chopped parsley
salt and pepper to taste
3 tablespoons (3¾) grated cheese

Cook the macaroni in boiling salted water as described on page 23. While it is cooking, heat the oil, add the pine nuts and chilli and fry gently. When the pine nuts begin to change colour, discard the chilli, stir in the brandy, raise the heat and stir continuously for 1 minute. Take from the stove, add parsley, salt and pepper. Drain the macaroni, return it to the pan or turn it into a hot dish. Add the sauce, stir gently but well and sprinkle with cheese.

MACARONI WITH BROCCOLI

¾ lb macaroni (mezze maniche)
1 lb broccoli
salt
2–3 tablespoons oil

1 medium-sized onion, chopped
1 oz pine nuts
about 1 tablespoon raisins or
  sultanas

Wash and trim the broccoli, discard any coarse stalks and cook in boiling water until tender. Drain but reserve the liquid. Break the broccoli into small pieces. Put aside.

Put the broccoli liquid into a large pan and add enough water to almost fill the pan. Add salt and the macaroni and continue cooking as described on page 23. In the meantime heat the oil, add the onion and cook until it begins to change colour. Add the pine nuts, raisins or sultanas and finally the broccoli flowerets. Stir gently and simmer until the macaroni is ready.

Drain the macaroni and return it to the pan, add the sauce, stir gently and then continue to cook for 3 minutes. Turn into a hot dish and serve at once.

LITTLE BOWS WITH PAPRIKA SAUCE

1 lb little bows (farfalle tonde)   *½ pint (1¼ cups) thin cream*
3 oz (6 tablespoons) butter   *grated cheese*
1–2 teaspoons (1¼–2½) Hungarian
  paprika

Cook and drain the little bows in boiling salted water as described on page 23. While it is cooking, heat the butter in a large casserole which can later be brought to the table. Add the paprika, stir it well into the butter, then add the drained little bows. Stir gently but well. Add the cream, stir gently again and continue cooking for 2–3 minutes, just long enough to heat the cream. Serve with grated cheese.

The quality of paprika varies considerably. The better the quality the less you will need.

LITTLE BOWS WITH FRANKFURTER SAUSAGES

1 lb little bows (cravattine)   *2 oz (4 tablespoons) butter*
6 frankfurters, sliced   *grated cheese to taste*

Cook the little bows in boiling salted water as described on page 23. Gently heat the butter in a large casserole, add the frankfurters and fry them for a few seconds, stirring frequently. Quickly drain the little bows, add to the pan, stir twice and serve at once, with cheese separately.

LITTLE QUILLS WITH A CHEESE SAUCE

1 lb little quills or nibs (pennini)
4 tablespoons (5) grated Pecorino
cheese
4 tablespoons (5) grated Parmesan
cheese

2 oz (4 tablespoons) butter
2 large ripe tomatoes
¼ teaspoon (⅓) dried oregano or
marjoram
salt and pepper to taste

Chop the tomatoes and rub through a coarse sieve. Cook the little quills in boiling salted water as described on page 23. Drain. Heat the butter in a large casserole, add the drained quills and stir gently. Add the tomato, stir again. Take from the heat, add the two cheeses, oregano, salt and pepper. Stir gently and serve at once.

Although in this recipe Pecorino and Parmesan cheeses are recommended, where these are not available, other hard, sharp cheeses can be substituted.

QUILLS WITH A DRIED MUSHROOM SAUCE

1 lb quills or nibs (penne)
1 oz (1 cup) dried mushrooms
1 oz (2 tablespoons) butter
1 large onion, finely chopped

6 thin strips bacon, diced
½ pint (1¼ cups) thin cream or top
of the milk
salt and pepper to taste

Soak the mushrooms in tepid water for 20 minutes, drain and finely chop. Heat the butter and gently fry the onion; add the bacon, raise the heat and stir, cook for 2–3 minutes, add the mushrooms, cream, salt and pepper and continue cooking for 15 minutes.

Cook the quills in boiling salted water as described on page 23. Drain and return them to the hot pan or turn into a hot dish, add the sauce, stir and serve at once.

SPIRALS WITH A MUSHROOM SAUCE

1 lb spirals (eliche)
1 oz (1 cup) dried mushrooms
2 oz (4 tablespoons) butter
1 tablespoon (1¼) finely-chopped
  parsley

¼ pint (⅔ cup) thin cream
salt and pepper to taste
grated cheese to taste

Soak the mushrooms in lukewarm water for 20 minutes, drain
and chop. Melt the butter in a small pan, add the mushrooms and
cook over a low heat for 5 minutes. Add the parsley, cream and
seasoning and cook another 6–7 minutes.

In the meantime, cook the eliche in boiling salted water as
described on page 23. Quickly drain and return to the pan or
turn into a hot dish, add the sauce, stir and serve with grated
cheese separately.

CHAPTER FIVE

BAKED

STUFFED MACARONI

Use the larger forms of pasta for this recipe, such as lumaconi, snails; cannelloni, large round tubes; rigatoni, ridged macaroni or mezze maniche, half tubes.

½ lb macaroni
3 tablespoons (3¾) olive oil
1 small onion, chopped
1 medium-sized can peeled tomatoes, chopped
salt
1 clove garlic
½ lb cream cheese

5 tablespoons (6¼) grated hard cheese
½ lb cooked ground meat
pepper and nutmeg to taste
2 eggs
3 tablespoons (3¾) approximately milk
1 oz (2 tablespoons) butter

Sauce Heat the oil and fry the onion until soft. Add the tomatoes and salt and cook for 15 minutes. Add the garlic and cook quickly for 5 minutes. Discard the garlic. Put the mixture aside but keep hot.

Stuffing Beat the cream cheese until smooth or rub it through a sieve. Combine with the grated cheese, meat, salt, pepper, nutmeg and eggs. Mix to a paste and add enough milk to moisten the mixture.

Cook the macaroni in boiling salted water as described on page 23. Drain and spread it out on a damp cloth. Cool, then put a little of the stuffing into each pasta shape. Rub a baking dish with butter, add the stuffed macaroni, cover with the sauce and bake in a hot oven (425°F., mark 7) for 15–20 minutes.

MACARONI AND MEAT CUSTARD

½ lb macaroni (zita)
½ lb cold diced cooked meat
1 oz (2 tablespoons) butter or other fat
1 large onion, finely chopped

salt and pepper
3 eggs
1 pint (1¼) milk
grated cheese

Cook the macaroni in boiling salted water as described on page 23. In the meantime prepare the remaining ingredients. Heat the butter, add the onion and cook gently until it is soft. Add the meat (this can be ham, cold roast meat, etc.) and cook until it begins to brown. Drain the macaroni and turn into a baking dish. Add the meat and onion, salt and pepper. Beat the eggs with the milk and stir gently into the macaroni and meat. Sprinkle with grated cheese and put the dish into a pan with enough warm water to come half-way up the sides. Bake in a moderate oven (350°F., mark 4) for 45 minutes.

MACARONI AND CHEESE CUSTARD

½ lb large elbow-shaped macaroni (tortiglioni)
1½ pints (3¼ cups) milk
4 eggs
salt and pepper

pinch grated nutmeg
½ lb (2 cups) finely-grated hard cheese
butter for greasing

Cook the macaroni in boiling salted water as described on page 23. While it is cooking, scald the milk. Beat the eggs thoroughly, add the scalded milk, mix well, add salt, pepper and nutmeg, and finally the cheese. Drain the macaroni. Rub a round, deep baking dish with butter. Add the macaroni and the egg and cheese mixture and stir gently. Put the dish into a pan with enough warm water to come half-way up the sides, and bake in a moderate oven (350°F., mark 4) for about 45 minutes or until the custard has set. Serve hot.

MACARONI WITH MUSHROOMS
AND TOMATOES

½ lb macaroni (tortiglioni, sedani)   salt and pepper to taste
½ lb fresh mushrooms, cleaned and   1 cup (1¼) hot water or stock
   sliced   butter for greasing
4 tomatoes, peeled and chopped   ½ pint (1¼ cups) Béchamel sauce
¼ cup (⅓) olive oil   (see page 138)
2–3 sprigs parsley, finely chopped   grated hard cheese to taste

Heat the oil, add the mushrooms, tomatoes, parsley, salt and pepper and cook for a few minutes, stirring all the time. Add the hot water, stir and continue cooking over a low heat until the tomatoes are soft.

In the meantime, cook the macaroni in boiling salted water as described on page 23. Make the Béchamel sauce. Drain the macaroni. Rub a baking dish with butter and add the macaroni. Stir in first the mushroom and tomato sauce then, rather lightly, the Béchamel sauce. Add the grated cheese, salt and pepper and bake in a moderate oven (350°F., mark 4) for 20–30 minutes. Serve hot with grated cheese separately.

Left-over boiled pasta also can be used in this way.

MACARONI WITH AUBERGINE AND
TOMATO SAUCE

½ lb spiral macaroni (eliche)   1 clove garlic, minced
1 lb aubergines (eggplants)   salt and pepper to taste
1 lb canned peeled tomatoes   5 tablespoons (6¼) milk
6 tablespoons (7½) olive oil   1 oz (2 tablespoons) butter
1 onion, minced   ½ cup (⅔) grated hard cheese
a little rosemary, fresh or dried

Heat 3 tablespoons (3¾) of oil, add half the onion, all the tomatoes and their liquid, rosemary, garlic, salt and pepper. Let this cook gently until the tomatoes are soft. As they cook, crush them. In another pan heat the remaining oil with the same quantity of water, add the remaining onion and cook gently. Peel the aubergines, cut into cubes, and add to the pan. Now add the milk, salt and pepper and simmer until the aubergines are soft.

Cook the macaroni in boiling salted water as described on page 23 but only for 7 minutes instead of the usual 10. Drain and quickly rinse in cold water. Drain again.

Rub a casserole with butter, cover the bottom with macaroni, add a few slivers of butter, half the tomato sauce, the whole of the aubergine mixture, then the remaining macaroni. Cover with the remaining tomato sauce. Sprinkle with cheese and dot with butter. Bake in a moderate oven (350°F., mark 4) for 20–25 minutes.

Although this dish is already substantial, the following addition makes it more so. Separate the yolks from the whites of 3 eggs. After the dish has been in the oven for 15 minutes, spread the egg whites over the top. These should not be beaten but just lightly enough whisked to break them up. Return the dish to the oven and continue baking until the whites are set. In the meantime, lightly beat the egg yolks, pour these over the egg whites and return the dish to the oven but without heat. Leave until the eggs are set, a matter of a few minutes.

MACARONI IN SCALLOP SHELLS

$\frac{1}{2}$ lb macaroni (pennini)
2 oz (4 tablespoons) butter
2 teaspoons (2$\frac{1}{2}$) plain flour
1–2 cups (1$\frac{1}{4}$–2$\frac{1}{2}$) stock

salt and pepper
4 tablespoons (5) grated cheese
extra butter
breadcrumbs

Cook the macaroni in boiling salted water as described on page 23. While the macaroni is cooking, heat the butter, add the flour, stir until the mixture is smooth, then gradually add enough stock to make a thick sauce. Add salt and pepper to taste and half the cheese. By this time the macaroni will be al dente. Drain and stir it gently into the sauce.

Rub 6 scallop shells with butter and fill with the macaroni

mixture. Top with the remaining cheese, dot with slivers of butter and sprinkle lightly with breadcrumbs. Bake in a hot oven (400°F., mark 6) for about 10 minutes or until the butter has melted and the top is browned.

MACARONI WITH ONION AND TOMATO SAUCE

½ lb macaroni (denti d'elefante)   salt and pepper
2 large onions, thinly sliced   1 teaspoon (1¼) sugar
4 large tomatoes, peeled and thinly butter for greasing
   sliced   ½–¾ lb thinly-sliced semi-soft
1 oz (2 tablespoons) butter   cheese
2 cloves garlic, finely chopped

Heat the butter in a pan, add the onions, let these fry gently until soft. Add the garlic, continue cooking until it begins to brown. Add the tomatoes, salt, pepper and sugar. Stir well and continue cooking for 20–25 minutes. While the sauce is cooking, cook the macaroni in boiling salted water as described on page 23. Drain and mix with the sauce.

Rub a deep baking dish with butter. Cover the bottom with a layer of the macaroni mixture. Now add a layer of cheese. Repeat this until all the ingredients are finished. The top layer must be of cheese. Bake in a moderate oven (350°F., mark 4) until the cheese browns and melts.

A good soft cheese which melts easily is essential for this dish.

MACARONI WITH GROUND MEAT

½ lb macaroni (zita)   salt and pepper
1 lb ground beef   1 pint (1¼) Béchamel sauce (see
¼ lb (1 cup) butter   page 138)
2 medium-sized onions, finely   1 egg
   chopped   ½ cup (⅔) grated cheese
1 large tomato, peeled and chopped

Prepare the filling: heat the butter, add the onions and cook until they begin to change colour and become soft. Add the meat and cook until brown, add the tomato, salt, pepper and ½ cupful of hot water. Cover the pan and cook very slowly until the meat is tender.

Make the Béchamel sauce.

Cook the macaroni in boiling salted water as described on page 23. Drain. Rinse it swiftly in cold water and drain again well.

Cover the bottom of a baking dish with half the macaroni, add all the meat with its sauce, half the Béchamel sauce, then cover with the remaining macaroni. Beat the egg into the remaining Béchamel sauce and add the cheese. Pour this mixture over the top of the macaroni, and bake in a moderate oven (350°F., mark 4) for about 20 minutes or until the top is nicely browned. Serve hot.

STUFFED MACARONI SHEPHERDESS STYLE

½ *lb macaroni (millerighe)*	2 *tablespoons* (2½) *olive oil*
½ *lb spinach or beet leaves*	*salt, pepper, grated nutmeg*
¼ *lb curd cheese*	*butter for greasing*
1 *large egg, beaten*	½ *cup* (⅔) *single cream or milk*
3 *oz* (1 *scant cup*) *grated cheese*	

Stuffing Wash and cook the spinach or beet leaves until tender and drain quite dry. Chop finely and mix with the curd cheese, the egg, half the grated cheese, oil, salt, pepper and nutmeg.

Cook the macaroni in boiling salted water as described on page 23. Drain and place them on a damp cloth to dry. Fill each one with some of the stuffing. Rub a baking dish generously with butter and add the stuffed macaroni. Combine the cream with the remaining cheese and pour it over the top. Dot with a few slivers

7. Noodles with Brandy Raisin Sauce

8a. Noodles with a Piquant Sauce

8b. Spaghetti with an Uncooked Tomato Sauce

9a. Macaroni with a Pine Nut Sauce

9b. Stuffed Macaroni Shepherdess Style

10a. Macaroni with Broccoli

10b. Spaghetti and Sweet Pepper Salad

of butter and bake in a very hot oven (450°F., mark 8) for 15–20 minutes. Serve from the baking dish.

Canned or frozen spinach may be used in this recipe. Also lumaconi and mezze maniche can be stuffed in the same way.

MACARONI AU GRATIN

½ lb short macaroni (denti d'elefante)
1½ lb aubergines (eggplants)
1½ oz (3 tablespoons) butter
½ cup (⅔) oil
1 small onion, finely chopped

1–2 cloves garlic, finely chopped
salt and pepper to taste
¼ lb mozzarella cheese
1 cup (1¼) thin cream
fine breadcrumbs
extra butter

Peel the aubergines and cut into small cubes. Put into a colander or large sieve, sprinkle with salt, cover with a plate, add a weight and leave for about 1 hour to let out the bitter liquid.

Heat the butter and oil together in a pan, add the onion and garlic and fry until they begin to change colour. Rub the drained aubergines on kitchen paper until dry, add to the pan, add salt and pepper, cover the pan and cook gently until the aubergines are soft.

In the meantime cook the macaroni in boiling salted water as described on page 23. Drain and immediately drop into cold water. Drain again. Put about half the macaroni in an oven-proof casserole, add half the aubergine sauce and a layer of mozzarella. Add the remaining macaroni, sauce and mozzarella. Add the cream, sprinkle generously with breadcrumbs and slivers of butter and cook in a hot oven (425°F., mark 7) for about 1 hour.

Serve in the casserole in which the macaroni was cooked or, if preferred, gently turn it on to a large, deep platter as shown in the picture.

BAKED MACARONI WITH BOLOGNESE SAUCE

$\frac{1}{2}$–$\frac{3}{4}$ lb macaroni shells (abissini)
Bolognese sauce (see page 129)
$\frac{1}{2}$ pint (1$\frac{1}{4}$ cups) cream

grated hard cheese to taste
1 oz (2 tablespoons) butter

First prepare the sauce. When this is ready, cook the macaroni in boiling salted water as described on page 23 but for 1 minute less. Drain, rinse swiftly in cold water and drain again. Put into a baking dish. Mix the cream with the sauce, stir this into the macaroni. Sprinkle with cheese, dot with slivers of butter and put into a hot oven (400°F., mark 6) for about 5 minutes. Serve at once, with grated cheese separately.

GNOCCHI WITH CREAM AND PARMESAN CHEESE

1 lb gnocchi
1 pint (2$\frac{1}{2}$ cups) cream

$\frac{1}{2}$–1 cup ($\frac{2}{3}$–1$\frac{1}{4}$) grated Parmesan cheese

Cook the gnocchi in boiling salted water as described on page 23. Drain and turn quickly into a shallow baking dish. Add the cream, sprinkle with Parmesan and bake in a hot oven (400°F., mark 6) for about 15 minutes. Serve hot.

MACARONI AU GRATIN

½ lb macaroni (ricciutelle or
  eliche)
1 oz (2 tablespoons) butter
2 tablespoons (2½) grated cheese
¼ lb soft cheese, thinly sliced
1 cup (1¼) canned peeled tomatoes,
  chopped

salt and pepper to taste
6–8 small black olives, stoned and
  chopped
finely-chopped oregano or
  marjoram to taste
3 tablespoons (3¾) olive oil
fine breadcrumbs

Cook the macaroni in boiling salted water as described on page 23, but for 2 minutes less. Drain, turn into a baking dish, add the butter and grated cheese and mix well. Cover with the soft cheese, spread with tomatoes, and sprinkle with salt, pepper, olives, oregano, oil and finally breadcrumbs. Bake in a hot oven (450°F., mark 8) for 10 minutes. Serve at once.

CASSEROLE OF MACARONI AND HARD-BOILED EGGS

½ lb macaroni (ricciutelle)
6–8 hard-boiled eggs, thinly sliced
1 pint (1¼) Béchamel sauce (see
  page 138)

butter
¼ lb grated hard cheese
finely-chopped sweet pepper to
  taste

Make the Béchamel sauce. Cook the macaroni in boiling salted water as described on page 23. Drain. Rub a baking dish with butter. Cover the bottom with a layer of macaroni, add a layer of sliced eggs, sprinkle with cheese and some chopped sweet pepper. Continue in this manner until these ingredients are finished. Add the sauce, stir gently to make sure it penetrates to the bottom of the dish. Bake for about 20 minutes in a moderate oven (350°F., mark 4) or until the top is brown.

  Instead of sweet peppers, cooked peas may be used, or chopped tomato, or croûtons, or all of these ingredients combined.

BAKED MACARONI WITH PEAS

½ lb macaroni (farfalle, etc.)
1 lb fresh peas, shelled
¼ cup (⅓) melted butter
1 large finely-chopped onion

finely-chopped garlic to taste
2–3 sprigs parsley, minced
salt and pepper

Cook the peas in salted water to cover until tender. Drain. Heat the butter, add the onion and garlic and simmer until the onion is soft. Add parsley, salt and pepper. While these ingredients are cooking, cook the macaroni in boiling salted water as described on page 23. Drain and turn into a casserole. Add the peas and the onion sauce, stir gently but well. Bake in a moderate oven (350°F., mark 4) for 15 minutes.

If fresh peas are not available, use frozen garden peas.

MACARONI WITH ONION SAUCE

½ lb macaroni (bucatini)
4 onions, about 1 lb, finely sliced
3–4 tablespoons (3¾–5) each olive
  oil and water

salt and pepper to taste
1 cup (1¼) grated cheese

Heat the oil and water, add the onions and cook gently until soft. Season. Cook the macaroni in boiling salted water as described on page 23. Drain, return to the pan, mix in the onion sauce, turn into a baking dish, sprinkle with cheese, stir gently and bake in a hot oven (425°F., mark 7) for 5–10 minutes.

MACARONI WITH HAM AND CHEESE

½ lb short macaroni (denti
  d'elefante)
½ lb cooked ham, diced
2 oz (⅔ cup) grated cheese
butter for greasing

salt and pepper
2 eggs
1 pint (2½ cups) milk
fine breadcrumbs

Cook the macaroni in boiling salted water as described on page 23. Rub a casserole with butter. Drain the macaroni and arrange a layer on the bottom of the casserole. Sprinkle with a layer of ham and cheese, add another layer of macaroni, season lightly, cover with ham and cheese, and spread with the remaining macaroni. Beat the eggs. Scald the milk, stir in the eggs and pour this over the top. Sprinkle the top with breadcrumbs and dot with slivers of butter. Bake in a moderate oven (350°F., mark 4) for 20 minutes.

CASSEROLE OF NOODLES AND VEGETABLES

$\frac{1}{2}$ lb narrow flat noodles (tagliatelle, fettuccine, etc.)
salt
about 1$\frac{1}{2}$ lb potatoes
about 1$\frac{1}{2}$ lb firm cabbage

$\frac{1}{4}$ lb (1 cup) butter or other fat
1 large onion, thinly sliced
sage to taste
$\frac{1}{2}$–1 cup grated hard cheese
$\frac{1}{2}$ lb soft cheese, very thinly sliced

Large potatoes are the best for this recipe. Have ready a large pan with plenty of boiling salted water. Peel the potatoes, cut into thick rounds or cubes and add to the pan. Wash and shred the cabbage, add to the pan and continue cooking until the potatoes are almost cooked. Add the noodles and cook for the prescribed time.

In another pan, heat the butter and fry the onion until soft. Add the sage and the grated cheese. Cook gently to a sauce, stir well. Discard the sage.

Drain the noodles and vegetables. Arrange a layer of noodles and vegetables at the bottom of a baking dish. Add a layer of onion and cheese sauce, and another of sliced soft cheese. Repeat these layers until all the ingredients are finished, the top layer being one of noodles and vegetables. Put the casserole in a hot oven (450°F., mark 8). After 5 minutes turn off the heat and leave it for about 15 minutes to settle without becoming over-cooked or dry.

NOODLE RING

½ *lb flat noodles (tagliatelle)*
1 cup (1¼) thick cream
3–4 eggs, lightly beaten

butter for greasing
fine breadcrumbs

Cook the noodles in boiling salted water as described on page 23. Drain. Mix with the cream and eggs. Rub a ring mould generously with butter and sprinkle lightly with breadcrumbs. Add the noodles. Set the pan in another pan with hot water and bake in a moderate oven (350°F., mark 4) for 45 minutes or until set. Unmould to serve. Fill the centre with creamed fish, chicken or hard-boiled eggs.

DEVILLED SPAGHETTI

½ *lb spaghetti*
4 oz (1 cup) cooking fat
½ *lb fresh mushrooms, sliced*
1 onion, finely chopped
1 clove garlic, crushed
1 lb peeled chopped tomatoes

salt and pepper to taste
cayenne pepper to taste
2 teaspoons (2½) sugar
1 cup (1¼) diced cooked chicken or ham
grated hard cheese

Heat the fat and fry the mushrooms until tender. Put these aside and, in the same fat, fry the onion and garlic until soft but not brown. Discard the garlic. Add the tomatoes, salt, pepper, cayenne pepper (be generous with the pepper for this dish should have a good piquant flavour), and sugar. Cook this over a good heat until the mixture is boiling. Add the diced chicken and mushrooms. Put aside but keep warm.

Cook the spaghetti in boiling salted water as described on page 23. Drain and turn into a baking dish. Add the sauce and stir gently with a fork. Sprinkle generously with grated cheese. Bake in a moderate oven (350°F., mark 4) for 15–20 minutes.

BAKED SPAGHETTI WITH LAMB

½ lb spaghetti

½ lb (1 cup) ground meat,
    preferably lamb

2 oz (¼ cup) butter or lard

1 large onion, finely chopped

1 oz (¼ cup) pine nuts

salt and pepper

¼ teaspoon (⅓) cinnamon

1 cup (1¼) tomato juice

1 small can tomato paste

1 cup (1¼) water

grated cheese

First prepare the sauce. Heat the fat and fry the onion until tender. Add the meat and brown lightly. Add the pine nuts. Season with salt, pepper and cinnamon. Add the tomato juice and tomato paste diluted with the water. Cook gently on top of the stove for 30 minutes until the sauce thickens.

Break the spaghetti into 2-inch lengths and cook in boiling salted water as described on page 23. Drain. Stir the spaghetti into the sauce, mixing well. Turn into a baking dish, sprinkle with grated cheese and bake in a moderate oven (350°F., mark 4) until the cheese is melted. Serve hot.

A SPECIAL TIP FOR SOUFFLÉ RECIPES

To ensure that the soufflé in the following recipes does not 'flop' when taken from the oven, try the following: Mix 1 teaspoon (1¼) of dried yeast with ½ teaspoon (⅔) of sugar, and 1 tablespoon (1¼) of water. Leave for 10 minutes in a warm place. Add it to the Béchamel sauce after the egg yolks have been added. The yeast seems to give the soufflé a firmness which prevents that last-minute drop when taken from the oven. And do not fill the soufflé dish more than three-quarters full.

EMPRESS SOUFFLÉ

½ lb macaroni
1 pint (1¼) Béchamel sauce (see page 138)
salt, pepper and nutmeg
¾ lb soft cheese, diced
4 tablespoons (5) grated cheese

3 eggs, separated
butter for greasing
2–3 tablespoons (2½–3¾) single cream or top of the milk
¼ lb cooked ham, diced

Cook the macaroni in boiling salted water as described on page 23, but for 2 minutes less than recommended. Drain, pour cold water over it and drain again.

Prepare the Béchamel sauce (flavour with salt, pepper and freshly-grated nutmeg), add the diced soft cheese and half the grated cheese. Take from the heat and beat in the egg yolks, one at a time. Put aside but keep warm.

Rub a soufflé dish with butter, add the macaroni, cream, a few slivers of butter, the remaining grated cheese, the ham and half the Béchamel sauce. Stir lightly with a fork. Beat the egg whites until stiff and fold gently into the remaining Béchamel sauce. Pour this over the top of the macaroni and bake in a moderate oven (350°F., mark 4) for about 45 minutes or until the top is browned. Serve at once.

Instead of ham, thinly-sliced fresh or canned mushrooms may be used.

NOODLE CHEESE SOUFFLÉ

½ lb noodles (fettuccine)
4 tablespoons (5) grated Gruyère or Emmental
1 pint (1¼) Béchamel sauce (see page 138)

grated nutmeg
¼ lb soft cheese, diced
3 large eggs, separated
butter for greasing
¼ pint (⅔ cup) thin cream

First prepare the Béchamel sauce. While it is still hot, add a good sprinkling of freshly-grated nutmeg, the soft cheese, and 3 tablespoons (3¾) of the grated cheese. Stir it well until the cheeses have melted, then take the pan from the heat and beat in the egg yolks, one by one, until the sauce is thick and creamy. Put aside but keep warm.

Cook the noodles in boiling salted water as described on page 23 and drain.

Rub a soufflé dish with butter, add the cooked noodles and spread with cream, ½ oz (1 tablespoon) of butter, the remaining grated cheese, and half the Béchamel sauce. Stir gently with a fork. Beat the egg whites until stiff, fold (with a metal spoon) into the remaining sauce. Pour this over the noodles and bake in a moderate oven (375°F., mark 5) until the soufflé has risen and the surface is a golden brown.

Instead of yellow fettuccine, an equal quantity of mixed green and yellow may be used.

MACARONI SOUFFLÉ

½ lb macaroni (pennette, mezze penne or sedanini)
1¼ oz (2½ tablespoons) butter
1¼ oz (5 tablespoons) white plain flour
1 pint (2½ cups) milk

3 egg yolks, well beaten
3 egg whites, stiffly beaten
extra butter for greasing
4 oz (1⅓ cups) grated cheese
2 tablespoons (2½) finest bread-crumbs

Cook the macaroni in boiling salted water as described on page 23. Drain, rinse in cold water then drain again. Put aside.

Melt the butter, add the flour and stir until it is smooth. Continue cooking and stirring until the mixture is a light brown. Gradually add the milk (clear stock may be used instead) and, stirring all the time, cook to a thick smooth sauce. Take the pan from the heat and whisk in the egg yolks, return the sauce to the stove and, stirring continuously, cook for 1 minute. Take from the stove, beat well, then fold in the egg whites, using a metal spoon.

Rub a soufflé dish with butter. Add a layer of macaroni, sprinkle with cheese, add another layer of macaroni, another of cheese and then a final layer of macaroni. Pour the sauce over the top, sprinkle with breadcrumbs and slivers of butter. Bake in a moderate oven (350°F., mark 4) for 30–40 minutes or until the soufflé has risen and is brown on top. Serve hot.

BAKED LASAGNE (1)

½ lb wide lasagne
1 tablespoon (1¼) tomato paste
½ pint (1¼ cups) stock
2 tablespoons (2½) olive oil
1 onion, finely chopped
1 carrot, finely chopped
1 stalk celery, chopped

½ lb ground cooked meat
½ cup (⅔) white wine (optional)
salt and pepper
½ pint (⅔) Béchamel sauce (see page 138)
butter or other fat for greasing
grated cheese

Dilute the tomato paste with the stock. Heat the oil, add the onion, carrot and celery, cook until they begin to change colour, then add the meat. Continue cooking until this begins to brown, then add the diluted tomato paste. Cover and cook gently for 15 minutes. Add the wine (if using), salt and pepper and continue cooking until the vegetables are very soft.

Make the Béchamel sauce. Put aside but keep warm.

Cook the lasagne in boiling salted water and drain as described on page 24.

Rub a square baking dish generously with butter and spread a layer of the cooked lasagne at the bottom. Cover this with some of the meat and vegetable sauce, then with a layer of Béchamel and sprinkle with grated cheese. Repeat these layers until all the ingredients are used up. The top layer should be one of cheese. Bake in a moderate oven (350°F., mark 4) for 30–45 minutes or until the top has browned.

BAKED LASAGNE (2)

$\frac{1}{2}$ lb lasagne

2 tablespoons ($2\frac{1}{2}$) olive oil

1 lb ground meat

1 onion, minced

1 clove garlic

4 tablespoons (5) tomato paste

2 cups ($2\frac{1}{2}$) water

salt and pepper

$\frac{3}{4}$ lb soft cheese

butter for greasing

grated hard cheese

The lasagne can be either green or white, or half and half. The meat pork or beef, or a mixture of both. The size of the onion is a matter of taste.

Heat the oil and add the meat, onion and garlic. Stir well. Fry until brown. Discard the garlic. Dilute the tomato paste with the water. Add to the pan with salt and pepper. Cover and cook gently for 1 hour.

Cook the lasagne in boiling salted water and drain as described on page 24.

Slice the soft cheese as thinly as possible. Rub an oblong or square casserole with butter. Arrange a layer of the drained lasagne on the bottom. Spread with a layer of the meat sauce and a layer of the soft cheese. Repeat until all the ingredients are used up, making sure that a layer of the meat sauce and soft cheese come last. Sprinkle with grated cheese and bake in a moderate oven (350°F., mark 4) for 30–45 minutes.

Instead of soft cheese, a thick white sauce (see page 138) can be substituted and layered in exactly the same manner. If using both green and white lasagne, use them in alternate layers.

BAKED LASAGNE BOLOGNA FASHION

$\frac{1}{2}$ lb lasagne squares

1 oz (1 cup) dried mushrooms

1 pint ($1\frac{1}{4}$) Béchamel sauce (see page 138)

1 recipe Bolognese sauce (see page 129)

3 oz (6 tablespoons) butter

1 clove garlic

1 cup ($1\frac{1}{4}$) milk

2–3 sprigs parsley, finely chopped

pinch salt

1 cup ($1\frac{1}{4}$) grated Parmesan cheese

Soak the mushrooms in tepid water, squeeze dry and chop them coarsely. Make a Béchamel and a Bolognese sauce. Cook and drain the lasagne in boiling salted water as described on page 24.

Heat one-third of the butter, fry the garlic until brown, then discard it. Add the mushrooms, milk, parsley and salt, stir and cook gently for 15 minutes.

Rub an oblong or square baking dish with butter. Cover the bottom with a layer of lasagne, spread it thinly with Béchamel sauce, then with Bolognese sauce. Sprinkle with grated Parmesan. Continue in this way until all the ingredients are used up, adding 2 layers of the mushroom mixture as well. The top layer should be lasagne, sprinkled with grated Parmesan and dotted with slivers of the remaining butter. Bake in a moderate oven (350°F., mark 4) for 30–45 minutes or until a light crust forms on the top.

Green lasagne is cooked in the same manner.

LASAGNE AND CREAM CHEESE

½ lb lasagne squares or oblongs
1 lb cream cheese
½ lb (2 cups) grated hard cheese
salt and pepper

3 eggs, well beaten
2 oz (4 tablespoons) butter
finely-chopped parsley or dill to taste

Rub the cream cheese through a sieve, add the grated cheese, salt, pepper and finally the eggs. Beat the mixture until it is smooth. Put aside.

Cook the lasagne in boiling salted water and drain as described on page 24.

Rub a square or oblong baking dish with butter. Spread a layer of lasagne at the bottom. Spread with the cheese mixture and sprinkle lightly with parsley. Repeat until all the lasagne is used up. The top layer should be of cheese sprinkled with parsley. Dot with slivers of butter. Bake in a moderate oven (350°F., mark 4) for 30–45 minutes or until the top is a golden brown.

If the cheese used in this recipe is rather dry, add a few tablespoonfuls of milk or cream, otherwise the lasagne could become dry.

GREEN AND WHITE CANNELLONI WITH A CHEESE SAUCE

¼ lb each green and white lasagne
  squares
¾ lb soft cheese, diced
1½ cups (scant 2) meat sauce (see
  page 131)

1 pint (2½ cups) thick white sauce
  (see page 138)
3 egg yolks
¼ lb cooked ham, diced
butter for greasing
grated cheese

Make the two sauces. First make the meat sauce, which can simmer while the white sauce and the lasagne are cooking. When the white sauce is cooked, take it from the heat and beat in the egg yolks, one at a time, then add the soft cheese and ham.

Rub an oblong or square baking dish with butter.

Cook the lasagne in boiling salted water and drain as described on page 24. When they are dry, spread each piece with white sauce filling, starting with the pieces first taken from the pan. Roll each piece up to form a cannelloni (which should be rather like a stuffed pancake in appearance) and put them in the dish, one green, one white, side by side. When they are all in the dish, spread with the hot meat sauce and bake in a moderate oven (350°F., mark 4) for about 30 minutes. Sprinkle generously with grated cheese immediately before serving.

Sizes of lasagne squares or oblongs vary considerably. If they are very large, they should be cut into halves after they are cooked and drained and before being made into cannelloni, otherwise too much pasta will have to be rolled up, thus making them too solid.

SPINACH AND CHEESE-STUFFED CANNELLONI

½–¾ lb cannelloni 'tubes'
2 lb spinach
½ lb cream cheese
butter for greasing
3 eggs, beaten

salt, pepper and nutmeg
grated hard cheese to taste
1 pint (1¼) Béchamel sauce (see
  page 138)

Wash the spinach and cook it in a large pan until tender (do not add any water, there is enough adhering to its leaves). When it is quite tender, drain it well in a colander. Heat a little butter in the same pan, return the spinach and gently cook it for 5 minutes. Take it from the pan and chop it finely. Add the cream cheese, mix well, then add the eggs to bind the mixture. Add salt, pepper and freshly-grated nutmeg to taste, and the grated cheese. Put this mixture aside but keep it warm.

Make the Béchamel sauce. Put aside but keep warm.

Cook the cannelloni tubes in the same manner as for lasagne squares, a few at a time in boiling salted water. As soon as they are cooked, take from the pan with a perforated spoon and drain on a damp cloth. When cool enough to handle, put a little of the filling into each tube.

Generously rub a shallow baking dish with butter and arrange the cannelloni in a single layer. Cover with the Béchamel sauce and dot with slivers of butter. Bake in a moderate oven (350°F., mark 4) for 30–45 minutes or until the top is a golden brown.

Serve with a bowl of grated cheese separately.

There are thinner cannelloni tubes on the market which do not need boiling. These are much easier to stuff with filling as they are stiff and hard. However, I find that they take much longer to bake, need plenty of sauce to help them cook, also they are never quite as tender as the boiled pasta.

Instead of Béchamel sauce, $\frac{1}{2}$ pint ($1\frac{1}{4}$ cups) of cream can be mixed with the cheese.

CANNELLONI STUFFED WITH SOFT CHEESE

$\frac{1}{2}$ lb lasagne squares or cannelloni   butter for greasing
   tubes   tomato sauce (see page 128)
$\frac{3}{4}$ lb soft cheese   grated hard cheese to taste

Cook the lasagne squares or the cannelloni tubes in boiling salted water and drain as described on page 24.

Slice the soft cheese as thinly as possible. Place a slice or two on each piece of lasagne (or push the cheese into the cannelloni) to make a filling; roll up each square tightly, like rolling a pancake. Generously rub a baking dish with butter and arrange the rolled-up cannelloni in one layer. Cover with tomato sauce, it is important that the cannelloni are well covered. Sprinkle generously with grated cheese and dot with butter. Bake in a moderate oven (350°F., mark 4) for 15–20 minutes.

MACARONI AND CAULIFLOWER CHEESE

½ lb short macaroni (penne or maccheroni)
1 large white or green cauliflower
½–1 cup (⅔–1¼) grated hard cheese
2 oz (4 tablespoons) butter
extra butter for greasing
2 eggs
1 cup (1¼) milk
salt

Trim the cauliflower and cook it in boiling salted water until tender. Drain and cool. Cook the macaroni in boiling salted water as described on page 23. Drain. Divide the cauliflower into flowerets. Heat the measured quantity of butter, add the cauliflower and fry gently until brown. Rub a baking dish with butter, add a layer of macaroni and dot with slivers of butter. Add a layer of cauliflower, then another of macaroni. There will be two or three layers of each. Beat the eggs into the milk, add salt and the cheese; pour this over the top and bake in a hot oven (400°F., mark 6) for 5–10 minutes. Serve at once.

MACARONI AND BACON CASSEROLE

½ lb macaroni (elbow, chifferoni, etc.)
4–6 strips bacon
2 cans condensed tomato soup
1 onion, minced
salt and pepper
¼–½ teaspoon (⅓–⅔) caraway or aniseed seeds
1 cup (1¼) grated cheese

Cook the macaroni in boiling salted water as described on page 23. While it is cooking, prepare the sauce. Combine the tomato soup, onion, salt, pepper and caraway, and bring gently just to the boil. Very lightly fry the bacon in its own fat. Drain the macaroni. Add with the cheese to the simmering sauce and mix well. Pour this mixture into a baking dish, cover with the bacon and bake in a hot oven (400°F., mark 6) for about 25 minutes. Serve at once.

MACARONI WITH MELTED CHEESE

*1 lb macaroni (farfalle tonde,
    ricciutelle, etc.)*

*½ lb coarsely-grated Gruyère cheese
    3 oz (6 tablespoons) butter*

Cook the macaroni in boiling salted water as described on page 23. Drain. Spread a layer in a warm baking dish, cover with a layer of grated cheese and dot with butter. Continue in this way until the macaroni and cheese are used up. Bake in a warm oven (325°F., mark 3) for 15 minutes or until the cheese has melted. Serve at once.

If the Gruyère cheese is very fresh, it is better to slice it wafer-thin.

BAKED MACARONI WITH HAM

*½ lb macaroni (ricciutelle)
½ lb cooked lean ham, diced
1½ oz (3 tablespoons) butter
2 large eggs, separated
½ cup (⅔) sour cream or natural
    yoghourt*

*salt, pepper and nutmeg
1 cup (1¼) buttered breadcrumbs
    (see page 139)
2–3 tablespoons (2½–3¾) melted
    butter*

Cook the macaroni in boiling salted water as described on page 23. Drain and immerse in cold water, draining it again well. Put into a bowl.

Cream 1 oz (2 tablespoons) of butter with the egg yolks. Add the cream, beat until the mixture is smooth, then add the ham. Season with salt, pepper and a good sprinkling of freshly-grated nutmeg. Mix this lightly into the macaroni. Beat the egg whites until stiff, and fold them into the macaroni using a metal spoon. Rub a baking dish with the remaining butter and sprinkle it with half the breadcrumbs. Turn the mixture into the dish, then add the melted butter and sprinkle with the remaining breadcrumbs. Bake in a moderate oven (350°F., mark 4) for 40–45 minutes or until the top is brown and crisp. The centre will be light and fluffy.

Ricciutelle is a light, delicate macaroni, therefore it is important to rinse in cold water to prevent further cooking.

BAKED MACARONI WITH COURGETTES

1 lb macaroni (ricciutelle)
1 lb courgettes (zucchini), thinly sliced
1 pint (1¼) Béchamel sauce (see page 138)
4 tablespoons (5) olive oil
1 large onion, thinly sliced
salt
1 oz (2 tablespoons) butter for greasing and dressing
¼ lb soft cheese, sliced
5 eggs, separated

First make the Béchamel sauce. Put it aside but keep warm. Heat the oil with 2 tablespoons (2½) of water. Add the onion, cook this for a few minutes, then add the courgettes and salt. Cover the pan and cook gently until the courgettes are soft. In the meantime, cook the macaroni in boiling salted water as described on page 23. Drain and rinse rapidly in cold water. Drain again (this cold draining is necessary with a light macaroni such as ricciutelle to prevent further cooking).

Rub a baking dish with butter, add the macaroni, dot with the remaining butter and add the cheese. Spread with a few table-spoonfuls of the sauce. Cover with the courgettes and their gravy, and the remaining Béchamel.

Bake in a hot oven (400°F., mark 6) for 10 minutes. Pour the egg whites over the top of the Béchamel. Bake for another 5 minutes until the egg white is set. Take the pan from the oven and turn off the heat. Break the egg yolks on the top of the egg white. Return the pan to the oven and leave for 5 minutes with the door open. This will set the yolks without their hardening. Serve at once.

SCALLOPED CHICKEN AND MACARONI

½ lb macaroni (chifferoni rigati,   salt to taste
chifferoni, maccheroni, etc.)   2 cups (2½) soft breadcrumbs
½ lb diced cooked chicken   extra butter
1 oz (2 tablespoons) butter   2 hard-boiled eggs, sliced
1 oz (¼ cup) plain flour   buttered breadcrumbs, about 1 cup
1 pint (1¼) milk or chicken stock   (1¼) (see page 139)

Cook the macaroni in boiling salted water as described on page 23. Drain. While it is cooking, prepare the remaining ingredients.

Melt the butter in a pan, add the flour and stir until the mixture is smooth. Gradually add the milk, stirring all the time until the sauce is thick. Add salt, chicken, soft breadcrumbs and finally the cooked macaroni. Rub a baking dish with butter, add a layer of macaroni and chicken mixture then a layer of sliced egg. Repeat this until all the ingredients are used up. Sprinkle with buttered breadcrumbs and bake in a moderate oven (350°F., mark 4) for about 30 minutes or until brown on top.

Ham or other cooked meat may be cooked in the same manner. Also a layer of canned, sliced mushrooms may be used, spread over the eggs.

MACARONI RING

½ lb macaroni   diced cooked ham to taste
1 pint (2½ cups) milk   1 cup (1¼) grated hard cheese
1 cup (1¼) soft breadcrumbs   salt and pepper
1 oz (¼ cup) butter   paprika pepper to taste
4 eggs, well beaten   filling (see below)

Cook the macaroni in boiling salted water as described on page
23. Drain and rinse quickly in cold water. Combine with the
remaining ingredients (except filling), mixing well. Pour into a
greased ring mould and place in a pan of hot water and bake in a
moderate oven (350°F., mark 4) for about 1 hour or until the
mixture has set. Carefully unmould and arrange on a round
plate.

Fill with cooked peas, or with mixed peas and diced cooked
carrots, moistened with cream, or with asparagus tips.

MACARONI AND CHICKEN PIE

Almost any of the small, thick macaroni shapes can be used in
this recipe, i.e., maccheroni or the somewhat thicker, ribbed
maccheroni rigati, sedani, denti d'elefante, etc.

½ lb macaroni	3 eggs, separated
1 lb cooked chicken, ground	butter for greasing
¼ lb cooked ham, ground	grated hard cheese
1 cup (1¼) thin cream or top of the milk	

Cook the macaroni in boiling salted water as described on
page 23. Drain. While the macaroni is cooking, combine the
chicken and ham. Add the cream. Beat the egg yolks thoroughly
and the egg whites until stiff. First add the egg yolks to the meat
mixture then, using a metal spoon, fold in the egg whites.

Rub a round baking dish generously with butter and spread
over the bottom in a thick layer half of the cooked macaroni.
Spread with the chicken and ham mixture and cover with the
remaining macaroni. Cover with foil and either steam on top of
the stove for 45 minutes, or place the baking dish in a pan containing enough hot water to come half-way up the sides of the
baking dish and bake in a moderate oven (350°F., mark 4) for the
same time. Serve sprinkled with grated cheese.

MACARONI AND MEAT CASSEROLE

¾ lb macaroni
1 lb lean meat, ground
butter
1–2 onions, finely chopped
1–2 large sprigs parsley, finely
  chopped

1 green pepper, seeded and diced
  (optional)
salt and pepper
hot stock or water
fine breadcrumbs

Melt 2 oz (4 tablespoons) of butter in a pan, add the onion and fry until soft. Add the meat, continue frying until this changes colour; add the parsley, sweet pepper, salt and pepper, cover with stock and cook gently until the meat is tender.

While the meat is cooking, cook the macaroni in boiling salted water as described on page 23. Drain and return to the pan and mix with 1 oz (2 tablespoons) of butter. Rub a large casserole generously with butter, spread half the macaroni on the bottom, spread the meat mixture over the top and cover with the remaining macaroni. Sprinkle with breadcrumbs, dot with slivers of butter, cover and bake in a hot oven (400°F., mark 6) for about 20 minutes.

This dish can be prepared some hours in advance and put aside until required for baking.

MACARONI WITH ONIONS

1 lb macaroni (abissini)
6 large onions
olive oil

finely-chopped parsley to taste
salt and pepper
2 tablespoons (2½) tomato paste

Peel 5 onions and cook them in boiling salted water for 10–15 minutes. Rub a baking dish generously with oil. Drain the onions, cut each into half and arrange in the baking dish. Sprinkle with parsley, salt, pepper and oil. Bake in a moderate oven (350°F., mark 4) for about 1 hour or until the onions are soft but still whole.

Make a sauce. Peel and slice the remaining onion and put in a
pan with 3 tablespoons (3¾) of oil and 2 (2½) of water. Cook
gently until soft. Mix the tomato paste with 4 tablespoons (5) of
water (or stock), add salt and pepper and stir into the simmering
onion. Continue cooking slowly for another 20 minutes.

Cook the macaroni in boiling salted water as described on
page 23 about 15 minutes before the baked onions are ready.
Drain, return to the pan and add the sauce. Take the onions from
the oven, arrange round the sides of a hot serving dish and pour
the macaroni with the sauce in the centre.

CHAPTER SIX

LEFT-OVERS

MACARONI WITH PORK

2 cups (2½) cooked macaroni
1 lb ground pork
butter for greasing and dressing
1 large onion, minced
½ lb peeled and cooked tomatoes, or
   equivalent canned

1 cup (1¼) grated hard cheese
salt to taste
1 teaspoon (1¼) sugar
fine breadcrumbs

Melt 1 oz (2 tablespoons) of butter. Add the onion, fry this until it begins to brown, then add the meat. Let this cook until it browns. Mix the macaroni with the tomatoes, cheese, salt and sugar, then add the fried onion and pork. Rub a shallow baking dish with butter and add the macaroni mixture. Cover lightly with breadcrumbs and dot with slivers of butter. Place in a moderate oven (350°F., mark 4) and bake for 20 minutes.

FRIED NOODLES

This is a type of Italian omelette or *frittata* and any type of left-over noodles can be used in its preparation.

about 2 cups cold left-over noodles
6 eggs
grated hard cheese to taste
olive oil

½ lb pork sausage meat
¼ lb soft cheese, thinly sliced
   (optional)

Cut the noodles into small pieces. Beat the eggs until smooth, add the grated cheese. Stir this mixture into the noodles. Heat 2 tablespoons (2½) of oil in a frying pan. Add the sausage meat and cook it over a moderate heat until it is browned and thoroughly cooked. In another and larger pan heat enough oil to cover the bottom, add half the egg and noodle mixture, spread with the sliced cheese, then the sausage meat, and finally add the remaining noodles. Fry over a moderate heat until the underneath is crisp and brown. Then put the pan under the grill and cook until the top is crisp and brown. Turn on to a hot serving dish and serve at once.

Failing sausage meat, skin some pork sausages, crumble the meat and use this instead.

SPAGHETTI FRITTERS

cooked left-over spaghetti   *oil for deep frying*
thick batter

It is not possible to give exact quantities as the ingredients are left-overs, but 1 cup (1¼) of batter plus 2 cups (2½) of chopped, cooked spaghetti makes 8 fritters about 2 in in diameter.

Any type of batter may be used in this recipe, i.e. made with eggs, milk and flour; with beer and flour, or with white wine and flour. If using plain flour, add a little baking powder.

Cut the spaghetti into small bits and mix with the batter. Heat the oil until very hot. Drop the spaghetti, a tablespoonful at a time, into the hot oil. Fry each fritter until brown underneath, turn and brown the other side. Serve at once.

If liked, the fritters can be served with grated cheese, or melted butter, or any of the pasta sauces. If the original spaghetti dish had plenty of flavour, the fritters can be served plain.

MACARONI AU GRATIN

For this, cooked, left-over macaroni with the tomato or white sauce, spaghetti, noodles or other pasta shapes may be used. Servings depend on the quantity of left-over pasta.

cold cooked macaroni
butter for greasing
tomato sauce or purée, or thick white sauce (see page 138), or thick canned soup such as mushroom, chicken, etc.

grated cheese
breadcrumbs

Butter a baking dish. Combine the macaroni with the chosen flavouring – it should be fairly liquid – and sprinkle with grated cheese and breadcrumbs. Bake in a moderate oven (350°F., mark 4) for 20–30 minutes.

BAKED MACARONI WITH A MUSHROOM SAUCE

2 cups (2½) cooked macaroni
mushroom sauce (see page 136)
1 oz (2 tablespoons) butter
1 pint (1¼) milk
3 eggs, well beaten
½ cup (⅔) soft breadcrumbs

2 cups (2½) diced cooked chicken or ham
1 good sprig parsley, minced
2 teaspoons (2½) minced onion
salt and pepper

Put the butter and milk in a pan and, stirring all the time, bring gently to the boil. Cool. Pour the milk over the eggs. Mix well, then add the remaining ingredients, except the mushroom sauce. Rub a baking dish with butter, add the macaroni mixture, place in a moderate oven (350°F., mark 4) and bake for 30–45 minutes or until set. Serve in the baking dish with the mushroom sauce separately.

NOODLE OMELETTE

3 servings:

about 2 cups chopped cooked   *2 oz (4 tablespoons) butter*
  noodles (tagliatelle)   *4 eggs*
fine breadcrumbs or plain flour   *grated hard cheese*

Coat the chopped noodles in fine breadcrumbs, shaking them until the coating is evenly distributed. Heat 1½ oz (3 tablespoons) of butter, add the noodles and fry them until crisp and golden.

Make the omelette. Whisk the eggs until just mixed. Heat the rest of the butter in a large pan. Spread the beaten egg over the bottom of the pan. Stir once or twice with a spatula and lift up the edges as the eggs begin to cook to let the uncooked egg run underneath. Shake the pan gently back and forth to prevent the omelette sticking.

When the omelette is cooked and soft on top, spread the noodles over one half and fold the other half over the top. Serve sprinkled with cheese.

The contrast in textures is interesting and extremely tasty.

MACARONI OMELETTE – ITALIAN STYLE

3 servings:

This is not an omelette in the conventional style but rather more like a Spanish omelette. Make it with left-over macaroni cut into small pieces, and measure it in a cup.

1 cup (1¼) left-over macaroni   *1½ oz (3 tablespoons) butter*
6 eggs   *a little finely-chopped parsley*
salt and pepper   *1–2 teaspoons (1¼–2½) grated*
1 tablespoon (1¼) water   *hard cheese*

Whisk the eggs lightly with salt, pepper and water. Heat the butter and lightly reheat the macaroni, add the parsley, cheese

and finally the eggs. Mix gently and cook until the eggs are set
and the underneath is brown. Brown the top under the grill.

MACARONI CHEESE

Any type of macaroni can be used in this dish, including zita,
chifferoni, bombolotti and tortiglioni. However, at least ½ lb of
cooked macaroni would be required to make a sizable dish.

cooked macaroni   1–2 onions, finely chopped
grated cheese   salt and pepper
butter for greasing and dressing   fine breadcrumbs
sliced tomatoes

Rub a baking dish generously with butter. Cover the bottom with
a layer of tomatoes. Sprinkle with the onion, salt and pepper. Add
a layer of macaroni, then repeat these layers until all the ingredients are finished. Sprinkle the top with cheese and breadcrumbs,
and thin slivers of butter. Cover and put into a slow oven (325°F.,
mark 3) and leave for about 1 hour.

If preferred, the onions can be first lightly fried in butter or
other fat until they are soft. It gives the dish a slightly different
and richer flavour. Be generous with the tomatoes and, if fresh
tomatoes are not available, use canned, plus their liquid. The
tomatoes are important as they provide the liquid to keep the dish
moist, without them it would be very dry.

FRIED NOODLES WITH SAUERKRAUT

left-over short noodles   fat
sauerkraut

Cook the sauerkraut until hot. In another pan heat a little fat, fry
the noodles until a golden brown, and spread over the top of the
sauerkraut. Diced fried bacon or ham can also be used in this
simple but satisfying country dish from Germany.

SPAGHETTI CREOLE STYLE

3–4 servings:

left-over spaghetti
2–3 strips fat bacon, diced
1–2 onions, minced
a little diced sweet pepper
  (optional)

½ lb ground meat
1 cup (1¼) canned tomatoes with
  their liquid
salt and pepper

At least ½ lb cooked weight of spaghetti should be used.

Fry the bacon in a casserole until its fat runs freely and the bacon is crisp. Take out the bacon and put aside. Add the onion and sweet pepper and fry until the onion begins to brown. Add the meat and fry this until brown, then add the tomatoes. Stir well and continue cooking for 15–20 minutes. Return the bacon to the pan, stir and add the spaghetti. Mix well and cook gently until the spaghetti is reheated. Add salt and pepper and serve.

CHAPTER SEVEN

SALADS

STUFFED SWEET PEPPERS

4–6 *sweet peppers*
2 *cups* (2½) *cooked macaroni*
  (*small shapes*)
1 *stick celery, diced*
½ *cup* (⅔) *diced cucumber*

diced sweet pepper to taste
diced hard cheese to taste
enough sweet pickle to flavour
mayonnaise, enough to moisten

Combine the last seven ingredients and chill them for several hours in the refrigerator. Wipe the peppers, slice off their tops and remove the core and seeds. Fill the stuffing into the peppers and serve.

Large, firm tomatoes can be stuffed in the same manner.

MACARONI AND FISH SALAD

¼ *lb cold cooked macaroni* (*small shapes*)
½ *lb cold cooked fish*
1 *tablespoon* (1¼) *capers*

1–2 *stalks celery, cut into thin rounds*
salt and pepper
mayonnaise or salad dressing
green or black olives (*optional*)

Combine the fish with the capers, celery, macaroni, salt and pepper, add enough mayonnaise to moisten. If using olives, add these last as a garnish. Serve on a bed of watercress, or with a lettuce salad.

The fish can be of one kind only or mixed. Any of the small macaroni shapes can be used in this recipe.

MACARONI SALAD

4 servings:

½ lb cold cooked macaroni (elbow, chifferi rigati, etc.)
2 cups (2½) diced cooked chicken, ham or other white meat
½ cup (⅔) salad dressing (see page 138)
1 tablespoon (1¼) minced onion

1–2 stalks celery, chopped
a little chopped sweet pepper or pimiento (optional)
salt and pepper
½–¾ cup (⅔–1) mayonnaise
lettuce

Mix the meat with the salad dressing, onion, celery, sweet pepper, salt and pepper. Chill. Mix the mayonnaise with the macaroni. Add the meat and vegetable mixture, stir gently and serve with lettuce.

MACARONI AND VEGETABLE SALAD

½ lb cooked macaroni (small shapes)
½ lb cooked peas
½ lb diced cooked carrots

1–2 stalks celery, cut into thin rounds
salt and pepper
½ cup (⅔) salad dressing or mayonnaise

Combine the peas, carrots, celery, salt and pepper, add the macaroni and mix gently. Add the dressing – the exact quantity depends on taste but obviously the salad should not swim in dressing.

This salad can be served as it is or with lettuce or watercress.

MACARONI SALAD

½ lb cooked macaroni (small shapes)
mayonnaise

sliced hard-boiled eggs
peeled tomatoes
salt, pepper and paprika pepper

Mix the macaroni with enough mayonnaise to moisten it. Garnish with sliced hard-boiled eggs and tomatoes. Sprinkle with salt, pepper and paprika pepper.

Cooked peas, chopped green beans or diced carrot can be mixed into the macaroni before adding the mayonnaise.

MACARONI SALAD WITH VEAL OR CHICKEN

½ lb cooked cold short macaroni shapes
1–2 stalks celery, diced
sweet pickles to taste

1½–2 cups diced cooked veal or chicken
mayonnaise

Combine the first four ingredients, then add enough mayonnaise to moisten.

Diced cooked ham, cold mutton or beef may be used instead of veal or chicken.

SPAGHETTI SALAD

½ lb cooked cold spaghetti
chopped pickled cucumber or gherkins to taste

1–2 cups cooked peas
1 firm apple, diced

Combine the ingredients.

To the above mixture can be added a little mayonnaise to moisten it or some horseradish sauce. Also diced, cold cooked meat, such as chicken or ham, or mortadella, or thinly-sliced frankfurter or Vienna sausages.

GNOCCHI AND VEGETABLE SALAD

½ lb cooked gnocchi or shell-shaped pasta
½ lb cooked peas, fresh, frozen or canned

½ lb cooked chopped carrots
1–2 stalks celery, finely sliced
salt and pepper
about 1 cup mayonnaise

Combine the gnocchi with the vegetables, add salt and pepper to taste and mix well. Add the mayonnaise (or salad dressing, if preferred) and mix well.

This salad can be garnished with chopped hard-boiled eggs.

SPAGHETTI AND SWEET PEPPER SALAD

½ lb spaghetti

1 small yellow pepper

1 small red pepper

1–2 firm red tomatoes

4–6 anchovy fillets

coarsely-chopped parsley and basil

3–4 tablespoons olive oil

garlic, finely chopped, to taste

salt and plenty of pepper

Cook the spaghetti in boiling salted water as described on page 23. While it is cooking prepare the remaining ingredients.

Cut the peppers into halves. Remove the seeds and cores. Spear the pepper pieces on a long kitchen fork and hold them over a fairly high flame until the skin begins to blister. When all four pieces are blistered, pull off the thin skin and cut the flesh into thin strips. Drop the tomatoes into boiling water and leave for a few minutes or until their skins pull off easily. Cut the tomatoes into thin strips. Chop the anchovy fillets finely and mix into the chopped herbs and garlic. Combine all these ingredients, add salt, pepper and the olive oil.

Drain the spaghetti and drop at once into a bowl of cold water. Quickly drain and put into a deep bowl. Add the sweet pepper sauce, toss gently and serve.

CHAPTER EIGHT

SAUCES, DRESSINGS, STUFFINGS

TOMATO SAUCE (PLAIN)

1 lb canned peeled tomatoes
2 tablespoons (2½) olive oil
1 small onion, finely chopped
a pinch rosemary

1 teaspoon (1¼) sugar
1 clove garlic, crushed
salt and pepper to taste
2 tablespoons (2½) milk

Heat the oil with the same quantity of water, add the onion and cook this gently until soft. Add the tomatoes, slightly raise the heat and cook them until mushy, stirring from time to time. Add the rosemary, sugar, garlic, salt, pepper and milk and cook for 3 minutes, stirring all the time.

TOMATO SAUCE (RICH)

1 lb canned peeled tomatoes
2 oz (4 tablespoons) butter
2 tablespoons (2½) olive oil
2 oz (4 tablespoons) bacon fat or minced fat bacon
1 each small onion, stalk celery, carrot, all finely chopped

1 clove garlic, finely chopped
2–3 sprigs parsley, finely chopped
½ cup (⅔) hot stock or water
salt and pepper
1 teaspoon (1¼) sugar

Heat the butter and oil together in a large pan, add the bacon and fry until the fat runs, add the onion and other vegetables, garlic and parsley. Mix well and fry gently for about 5 minutes. Add the stock and continue cooking slowly. In the meantime crush the tomatoes, add them to the pan, stir well, add salt, pepper and

11. Macaroni au Gratin

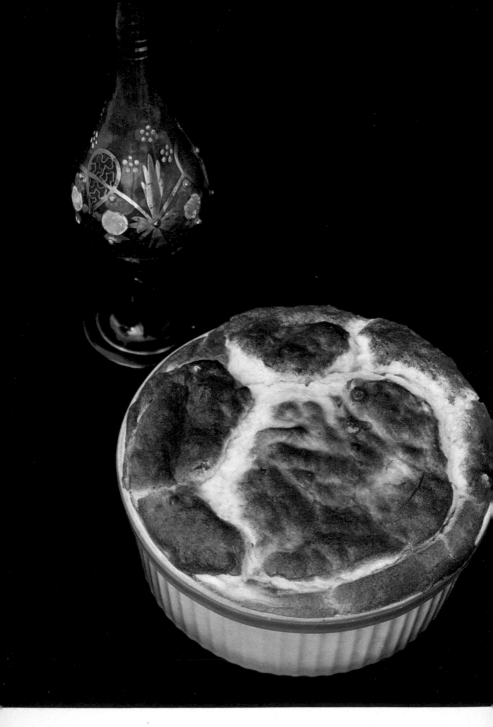

12. Empress Soufflé

sugar. Half-cover the pan and cook gently for 30–45 minutes, stirring from time to time.

This sauce can be served as it is, or rubbed through a sieve.

UNCOOKED TOMATO SAUCE

4 ripe peeled tomatoes   *1 stalk celery, chopped*
1 clove garlic   *3 tablespoons (3¾) grated cheese*
salt, pepper and sugar to taste   *2 tablespoons (2½) milk*
mixed green herbs to taste   *½ cup (⅔) olive oil*

Put the first seven ingredients into an electric blender and blend until smooth. Add the oil little by little as though making mayonnaise. Stir well and serve at once.

CREAM OF TOMATO SAUCE

1-lb can peeled tomatoes   *salt and pepper*
1 oz (2 tablespoons) butter   *1 teaspoon (1¼) sugar*
2 teaspoons (2½) plain flour   *½ cup (⅔) thin cream*

Rub the tomatoes with their liquid through a fine sieve. Heat the butter, stir in the flour and cook until it is smooth. Add the tomatoes, stirring all the time, and simmer for 20 minutes, stirring often. Add salt, pepper and sugar, stir well, take from the stove, add the cream and pour the sauce at once over the drained pasta.

This sauce is particularly suitable for the long pasta shapes, i.e. spaghetti, bucatini, tagliarelli, linguine and fettuccine.

BOLOGNESE SAUCE

A Bolognese sauce varies from cook to cook; even in Bologna there are a dozen different versions of this internationally-known sauce.

5

1 tablespoon (1¼) each butter and
   olive oil
1 tablespoon (1¼) chopped parsley
1 onion, chopped
¼ lb fresh mushrooms, chopped
¼ lb raw ground beef

½ cup (⅔) dry white wine
1 small can tomato paste
1 pint (1¼) clear meat stock,
   preferably chicken
1 teaspoon (1¼) sugar
salt and pepper

Heat the butter and oil together. Add the parsley and onion and
cook until the onion is a light brown. Add the mushrooms and
meat and cook gently for 3 minutes. Add the wine and continue
cooking until this has evaporated. Dilute the tomato paste with
some of the stock, add this to the pan, stir, then add the rest of the
stock. Add sugar, salt and pepper, again stir and continue to cook
slowly for 30 minutes.

MEAT SAUCE

1 lb lean beef, chopped
1 oz (1 cup) dried mushrooms
2 oz (4 tablespoons) butter
½ small onion, thinly sliced
½ clove garlic, crushed
1 stalk celery, finely chopped
1 medium-sized carrot, finely
   chopped

pinch rosemary (optional)
½ pint (1¼ cups) red wine, beer or
   stock
3–4 ripe peeled tomatoes
salt and pepper
½ pint (1¼ cups) water

Soak the mushrooms in tepid water for 20 minutes, squeeze dry
and drain. Heat the butter in a pan, add the meat and cook it
gently, stirring from time to time until it is brown all over. Add
the onion, garlic, celery, carrot, rosemary and mushrooms. Stir,
add the wine and cook for 15 minutes. Add the tomatoes, lower
the heat, add salt and pepper, cover the pan and cook gently
until the meat is very soft. Add the water, a little at a time to
prevent burning. When the sauce is ready, rub it through a coarse
sieve or purée it in a blender.

MEAT SAUCE FOR LASAGNE

1 lb (2 cups) ground meat (uncooked)	1 bay leaf
4 tablespoons (5) olive oil	a little rosemary (optional)
2 cloves garlic	1 sage leaf
1 medium-sized onion, minced	$\frac{1}{2}$ cup ($\frac{2}{3}$) red wine
1 medium-sized carrot, minced	1-lb can peeled tomatoes
1 stalk celery, minced	$\frac{1}{2}$ cup ($\frac{2}{3}$) milk
	salt and pepper

Heat the oil and add the garlic; when it is brown, take it from the pan and put aside. Add the onion, let this cook until soft but try to keep it from browning. Add the meat, fry this until it browns, stirring all the time to prevent it sticking together and forming lumps. Add the carrot, celery and herbs, stir well, then add the wine and cook gently for 10 minutes. Add the tomatoes plus their liquid, the milk, salt and pepper and cook gently for about 45 minutes.

Some cooks return the garlic to the pan with the salt and pepper, others feel they have enough flavour in their first cooking. It is a matter of taste but this sauce can certainly take a good flavour of garlic for those who like it.

SAUSAGE MEAT SAUCE

$\frac{1}{2}$ lb sausage meat, preferably pork	1 egg
3 tablespoons ($3\frac{3}{4}$) olive or other cooking oil	4 tablespoons (5) milk

Heat the oil in a frying pan, add the sausage meat, crumbling it well with a fork to separate it and prevent lumps from forming. Cook until it browns – this should be done slowly to ensure the meat is cooked through and not merely brown on top. Beat the egg into the milk. Stir this into the sausage meat, stirring the mixture well until the egg has set. Pour at once over cooked and drained spaghetti or similar long-shaped pasta.

HAM AND MUSHROOM SAUCE

¼ lb ham, thickly sliced and diced   3 tablespoons (3¾) olive oil
¼ lb fresh mushrooms, cleaned and   ½ cup (⅔) tomato paste
  thinly sliced   salt and pepper

Heat the oil and gently fry the mushrooms until they are soft.
Add the ham and continue cooking until this is hot; add the
tomato paste, diluted with 1 cup (1¼) of water, season with salt
and pepper and cook gently for 15 minutes.

BACON SAUCE

½ lb bacon   pepper
1–2 cloves garlic, chopped   salt (optional)

The bacon should have a fair amount of fat. Dice the bacon,
discarding the rinds (they can be used to flavour a stock). Fry the
bacon in a pan until the fat begins to run, add the garlic and
continue cooking until the bacon is crisp. Add pepper. Unless
the bacon is very mild, do not add salt. Take the bacon from the
heat, stir into hot spaghetti or other pasta shapes.
   Cheese should be used with this sauce.

CHICKEN LIVER SAUCE

½–1 lb chicken livers   ½ cup (⅔) dry sherry
plain flour   ½ pint (1¼ cup) chicken stock
2 oz (4 tablespoons) butter   finely-chopped parsley to taste
salt and pepper

Wash and clean the chicken livers. Pat dry on kitchen paper.
Chop coarsely and roll in flour. Heat the butter in a frying pan,
add the livers and cook gently for 5 minutes. Add salt and pepper,

stir, add the sherry and cook for 5 minutes. Add the stock and continue cooking for 15 minutes. Add parsley, stir and check for seasoning.

Serve with any pasta but this sauce is particularly good with the smaller shapes like gnocchi and abissini.

ANCHOVY SAUCE

8–12 anchovy fillets
2 tablespoons (2½) olive oil
1 clove garlic, crushed

2 tablespoons (2½) coarse dried breadcrumbs

Heat the oil and add the garlic. Cook until it begins to brown. Discard. Add the anchovies and cook until these are dissolved. Mash with a wooden spoon. Add the breadcrumbs, stir well and pour at once over cooked, drained pasta.

Pasta served with this sauce does not require the addition of cheese.

ANCHOVY AND TOMATO SAUCE

8–12 anchovy fillets
1 small can tomato paste
3 tablespoons (3¾) olive oil

1 clove garlic
pepper

Heat the oil and fry the garlic until it begins to brown. At this point it can be discarded if a mild flavour of garlic is preferred, otherwise leave it until the sauce is cooked and then discard it. Add the anchovy fillets and stir with a wooden spoon until they have dissolved. Add the tomato paste and pepper, stir well, cover the pan and cook slowly for 20 minutes.

Finely-chopped parsley also can be added at the same time as the tomato. This sauce is meant to be thick but, if a thinner sauce is preferred, add boiling water to dilute it.

Do not serve cheese with this sauce.

ANCHOVY SAUCE WITH GARLIC AND HARD-BOILED EGGS

8–12 anchovy fillets
2 cloves garlic, minced
3–4 hard-boiled egg yolks
¼ cup (⅓) olive oil

1 oz (2 tablespoons) butter
2 large sprigs parsley, minced
black pepper
juice ½ lemon

Heat the oil and butter together, add the garlic and cook this until it changes colour. Add the anchovies and cook gently until they are dissolved. Mix them well into the oil with a wooden spoon. While they are cooking, mash the egg yolks, add them to the pan, stirring well. Add the parsley and plenty of black pepper. Stir well and cook for 2 minutes. Take from the pan, add the lemon juice, stir again and serve at once.

TUNNY FISH SAUCE

½-lb can tunny (tuna) fish
2 tablespoons (2½) tomato paste
1 tablespoon (1¼) olive oil
1 clove garlic, crushed

good pinch dried rosemary or
    marjoram
pepper to taste

Dilute the tomato paste with ½ cupful of warm water (or stock if available). Drain and flake the fish. Heat the oil, add the garlic and cook until it begins to brown. Take out and discard. Add the fish, cook gently for 3 minutes, add the diluted tomato paste, stir, crush the fish and cook for 10 minutes. Add the rosemary and pepper, stir well and bring gently to the boil.

TUNNY FISH AND MUSHROOM SAUCE

½-lb can tunny (tuna) fish
1 oz (1 cup) dried mushrooms
3 tablespoons (3¾) olive oil

2 cloves garlic, finely chopped
1 cup (1¼) tomato paste
salt and pepper

Soak the mushrooms in warm water for 20 minutes. Squeeze dry, drain and chop finely. Flake the fish with a fork, discarding the liquid. Heat the oil, add the garlic and fry until it begins to brown. Add the mushrooms, stir, then add the tomato paste, with salt and pepper to taste. Cover and cook gently for about 20 minutes. Add the tunny fish, stir it well into the sauce; if the sauce seems too thick, add a little hot water and stir again.

If liked, finely-chopped parsley or other suitable green herbs, such as dill or fennel, can be added at the same time as the tunny.

LOBSTER SAUCE

1 medium-sized can lobster meat
3 tablespoons (3¾) olive oil
2 cloves garlic, crushed
1 large onion, finely chopped
4–6 ripe tomatoes, peeled and chopped

salt and pepper
chopped parsley to taste
1 pint (1¼) fish stock
1 tablespoon (1¼) tomato paste

Heat the oil and fry the garlic and onion until brown. Remove the garlic, add the tomatoes, salt, pepper and parsley. Simmer for several minutes, then add the fish stock. (If no fish stock is available, mix the juice from the lobster with enough hot water to bring it up to the required quantity. Dry white wine, dry cider or beer also can be added, but the quantity of liquid must remain the same.) Add the tomato paste. Cook over a low heat until the tomatoes are soft. Flake the lobster meat, add to the pan and continue cooking until this is hot but do not let it boil.

BUTTER, CREAM AND CHEESE SAUCE

3 oz (6 tablespoons) butter
½ cup (⅔) thin cream

4 tablespoons (5) grated hard cheese
1 teaspoon (1¼) plain flour

Heat half the butter in a small thick pan. Mix the flour and cream together, making sure there are no lumps. Add to the butter and stir over a low heat for a few minutes. Pour the sauce over the hot drained pasta, add the remaining butter and cheese.

This sauce can be served with any of the spaghetti shapes and in particular with a mixture of green and white fettuccine.

MUSHROOM SAUCE

1 lb fresh mushrooms
6 spring (green) onions
1 oz (2 tablespoons) butter
2 tablespoons (2½) olive oil

salt and pepper
2 tablespoons (2½) plain flour
1 pint (2½ cups) milk or cream

If necessary, wash the mushrooms but do not peel them. Pull off the stems (these can be used to flavour a soup). Thinly slice the mushroom caps. Slice the spring onions, using as much of the green part as possible.

Heat the butter and oil together. Add the onions and fry gently for 5 minutes. Add the mushrooms, salt and pepper. Cook for 10 minutes, stirring frequently. Add the flour and stir gently until this is blended into the mushroom mixture. Gradually add the milk or cream (or a mixture of both) and stir, bringing it all to boiling point. Cook over a low heat until the sauce is thick and make quite sure there are no floury lumps.

WALNUT SAUCE

¼ lb (2 cups) shelled walnuts,
    coarsely ground
2 oz (½ cup) pine nuts
1 small clove garlic

½ cup (⅔) olive oil
1 large sprig parsley
salt

Put all the ingredients into a blender and blend to a paste. Add 1-2 tablespoonfuls of water if a thinner sauce is preferred.

PESTO SAUCE

a good handful basil leaves
2–3 cloves garlic
3 oz (1 scant cup) grated Pecorino
  cheese

1 tablespoon (1¼) pine nuts
olive oil

Tear the basil leaves into pieces and pound them in a mortar with the garlic, cheese and pine nuts until the mixture is smooth. Gradually add, drop by drop, enough oil to make a thick but creamy sauce. Just before serving, add about 2 tablespoonfuls of the water in which the pasta has been cooking.

This sauce is a favourite in Liguria, especially in Genoa, and is served with trenette.

An imitation of this recipe can be prepared with parsley; and if Pecorino cheese is not easy to come by, use Parmesan cheese. This will be a good sauce but not a true pesto. Both sauces, however, go exceedingly well with almost any type of spaghetti and narrow flat noodles.

Pesto sauce can be bought bottled in Italian stores in Britain and the United States, and one Ligurian pasta manufacturer packages a jar of pesto with his trenette.

HERB SAUCE

3 tablespoons (3¾) olive oil
2 cloves garlic, finely chopped
2 tablespoons (2½) finely-chopped
  parsley

1 tablespoon (1¼) finely-chopped
  sweet basil or 1 teaspoon (1¼)
  dried
salt and pepper

Heat the oil and fry the garlic until it begins to change colour. Add the herbs, salt and pepper and simmer gently for about 5 minutes.

This sauce is best used with green pasta. It also adds greatly to the flavour if freshly-ground pepper is sprinkled generously over the pasta after the sauce has been stirred into it.

THICK WHITE SAUCE

1 oz (2 tablespoons) butter
1 oz (¼ cup) plain flour
½ pint (1¼ cups) hot water or milk
salt and pepper

Heat the butter in a saucepan, add the flour and stir well. Cook for 1 minute, stirring all the time. Still stirring, add the liquid and cook for 10 minutes. Add salt and pepper and beat thoroughly.

When 1 pint (2½ cups) of white sauce is called for, double the above quantities.

BÉCHAMEL SAUCE

This is made in the same manner as a white sauce (see above) but with milk instead of water. Sometimes a slice of onion is added, a little coarsely-chopped parsley, and a dash of freshly-grated nutmeg. This is then rubbed through a fine sieve and, if liked, a tablespoonful of cream can be added.

SALAD DRESSING

salt and pepper
1 tablespoon (1¼) white vinegar
3 tablespoons (3¾) olive oil
a little finely-chopped parsley or chervil (optional)

Combine a good pinch of salt and pepper in a salad bowl, add the vinegar and mix. Stir until the salt has dissolved. Add the oil and stir until this is completely incorporated into the dressing. Add the herbs. Stir well before adding to a salad or when serving separately.

The above recipe is basic. If making larger quantities, do so in the same proportion. If liked, a little dry mustard may be added to the dressing when adding the salt and pepper.

BUTTERED BREADCRUMBS

2 oz (4 tablespoons) butter   *6 oz (2½ cups approx) soft*
                                        breadcrumbs

Melt the butter in a frying pan. Add the breadcrumbs and cook them, stirring all the time until they are brown and all the butter is absorbed. They can be used at once or put into a jar, sealed and kept for a short time.

OIL, GARLIC AND CHILLI SAUCE

olive oil   *crushed chillies*
garlic

This recipe has no exact quantities and is only for those with a liking for strong flavours.

Heat a generous quantity of oil, add several minced cloves of garlic and as many coarsely-chopped chillies as the palate can take. Pour all this over cooked and drained spaghetti or similar shapes.

MEAT STUFFING FOR CANNELLONI AND OTHER LARGE PASTA SHAPES

½ lb lean ground meat   *½ cup (⅔) red wine (optional)*
1 thick slice bread   *½ lb (about 1 cup) cooked spinach*
2 oz (4 tablespoons) butter   *2 oz (⅔ cup) grated hard cheese*
1 small onion, minced   *salt and pepper*
stock or water   *2 eggs, beaten*

Soak the bread in water or milk until soft, then squeeze quite dry. Heat the butter, add the meat and onion, cook gently until it browns, then add enough stock to cover the bottom of the pan.

Cook gently for 20 minutes, add the wine (if using) and continue to cook until the meat is tender and all the liquid has evaporated. Rub through a mincer, then combine with the spinach, cheese, bread, salt and pepper. When blended, add the eggs to bind the mixture and use as required.

CHEESE FILLING FOR CANNELLONI AND LARGE PASTA SHAPES

$\frac{3}{4}$ lb (1$\frac{1}{4}$ cups) cream cheese
1 oz (2 tablespoons) butter
1 egg yolk
3 oz (1 scant cup) grated cheese

1 heaped tablespoon (1$\frac{1}{4}$) chopped
parsley
salt and pepper

Beat the butter until smooth, then add the egg yolk. Beat until creamy, then beat in the cream cheese and the grated cheese and continue beating until the mixture is smooth. Add the chopped parsley and season.

Enough for $\frac{1}{2}$ lb cannelloni tubes or lasagne squares.

CHAPTER NINE

SWEET DISHES

BAKED NOODLE PUDDING

½ *lb narrow flat noodles*
2 *oz (4 tablespoons) butter*
2 *eggs, well beaten*
¼ *lb (⅔ cup) seedless raisins*

1½ *oz (⅓ cup) mixed chopped peel*
2 *oz (4 tablespoons) white sugar*
¼ *teaspoon (⅛) powdered cinnamon*
butter or other fat for greasing

Cook the noodles in boiling lightly salted water as described on page 23. Drain, return to the pan, add the butter and mix well. Add the remaining ingredients in the order given, stir well, turn into a greased pie dish, cover and bake in a moderate oven (350°F., mark 4) for 20–30 minutes.

BAKED NOODLE CUSTARD

½ *lb noodles (tagliatelle)*
2 *pints (2½) milk*
4 *eggs, well beaten*

4 *oz (½ cup) sugar*
vanilla extract to taste
grated cinnamon to taste (optional)

Cook the noodles in lightly salted water as described on page 23 but for 2 minutes less than the recommended time. Drain and turn into a baking dish. While the noodles are cooking, cook the milk until it reaches blood heat. Beat the eggs with the sugar, add the vanilla and stir in the milk, adding cinnamon (if using). Pour this over the noodles, stir gently to let the liquid penetrate to the bottom of the dish. Bake in a low oven (300°F., mark 1) until the custard has set, about 1¼ hours. The custard should set so firm that a knife inserted in it comes out clean.

For those who use vanilla sugar, add this to the eggs instead of the extract. Cinnamon can be sprinkled lightly over the top of the custard or, if preferred, freshly-grated nutmeg can be used.

BAKED NOODLES WITH ALMONDS

½ lb noodles (tagliatelle or fettuccine)
¼ lb almonds
3 tablespoons (3¾) sugar

grated rind 1 lemon
butter for greasing
plain flour or fine breadcrumbs
sweet liqueur, any flavour

Cook the noodles in lightly salted boiling water as described on page 23. While they are cooking, blanch and peel the almonds. Chop finely. Combine the almonds, sugar and lemon rind, mixing well. Rub a shallow baking dish, preferably round, with butter and sprinkle with flour or fine breadcrumbs. Drain the noodles. Put a layer on the bottom of the buttered dish, sprinkle with the sugar and almond mixture and as much liqueur as the pocket or taste dictates. Add another layer of noodles, another of sugar and almonds and again liqueur. Repeat these layers until the ingredients are finished. The top layer should be of noodles. Now cover with foil or buttered paper. Put the dish into a pan with hot water to come half-way up the sides and bake in a moderate oven (350°F., mark 4) for 1 hour. Turn it out on to a serving plate and serve hot, sprinkled either with lemon juice or a little more liqueur.

NOODLES WITH HONEY

½ lb noodles (tagliatelle, fettuccine, etc.)
¼ lb honey

¼ lb (½ cup) butter
4 oz (1 cup) chopped walnuts

Cook the noodles in boiling lightly salted water as described on page 23. Drain and return them to the pan in which they were cooked. Add the butter and stir it well into the noodles. Add the nuts. In another and smaller pan, cook the honey until hot and runny. Pour it quickly over the noodles and serve at once.

LAYERED NOODLE PUDDING

$\frac{3}{4}$ *lb flat noodles (tagliatelle mezzane, fettuccine, etc.)*
3 oz (6 tablespoons) melted butter
$\frac{3}{4}$ *lb apricot jam*

sugar to taste
4 oz (1 cup) coarsely-ground walnuts

Cook the noodles in boiling lightly salted water as described on page 23. Drain and return to the hot pan. Add 2 oz. (4 tablespoons) of the butter. Put one-third of the noodles into a separate bowl. Mix this with jam, sugar and walnuts. Rub a baking dish with butter. Spread the bottom with half the plain noodles. Cover with the flavoured noodles, then add the remaining noodles and the rest of the butter. Put into a moderate oven (350°F., mark 4), cover and bake for 20 minutes. Serve in the baking dish.

NOODLES WITH WALNUTS

1 lb noodles (fettuccine, etc.)
4–6 oz (1–1$\frac{1}{2}$ cups) chopped walnuts
3 oz ($\frac{1}{3}$ cup) fine sugar

2 tablespoons (2$\frac{1}{2}$) melted butter
1 teaspoon (1$\frac{1}{4}$) strained lemon juice
1 teaspoon (1$\frac{1}{4}$) grated lemon peel

Cook the noodles as described on page 23 but in lightly salted boiling water. While they are cooking, prepare the sauce. Combine the walnuts and sugar. Drain the noodles and turn them into a hot serving dish. Add the butter, mix it well into the noodles, then stir in the lemon juice and peel. Gently stir with a fork until everything is well blended. Serve the walnut-sugar mixture sprinkled over the top.

NOODLES WITH POPPY SEEDS

This dish is prepared in the same manner as the preceding one, Noodles with Walnuts. Instead of walnuts, freshly-ground poppy seeds are used, and the quantity of butter is doubled.

Poppy seeds are usually available wherever spices are sold, and can be ground in a blender.

NOODLES WITH CREAM CHEESE

$\frac{1}{2}$ *lb wide noodles (tagliatelle,*
fettuccine, etc.)
$\frac{1}{2}$ *lb (1$\frac{1}{2}$ cups) cream cheese*
2 eggs, well beaten
2 tablespoons (2$\frac{1}{2}$) sugar

salt
butter
fine breadcrumbs
$\frac{1}{2}$–$\frac{3}{4}$ *cup* ($\frac{2}{3}$–1) *sour cream or*
natural unsweetened yoghourt

Cook the noodles in boiling lightly salted water as described on page 23. Drain and turn into a large warm bowl.

While the noodles are cooking, rub the cheese through a sieve into a bowl, add the eggs and beat the mixture until smooth and creamy. Add the sugar and a pinch of salt. Pour this mixture over the noodles. Mix lightly.

Butter a baking dish and sprinkle it all round with breadcrumbs. Add the noodles with their sauce. Spread the top lightly with a little of the sour cream, then sprinkle generously with breadcrumbs. Bake in a moderate oven (350°F., mark 4) for 20–30 minutes. Cut into slices to serve, with the rest of the sour cream.

When mixing the cream cheese and eggs, a little vanilla flavouring may be added, also a few sultanas or seedless raisins. Instead of breadcrumbs, dry cake or biscuit crumbs may be used.

NOODLES WITH CURD CHEESE
AND WALNUTS

8 servings:

¾ lb noodles
1 lb cream cheese
¼ lb (1 cup) shelled and crushed
    walnuts
3 egg yolks
1 cup (1¼) thick cream
2–3 tablespoons (3¾) sugar
2 tablespoons (2½) seedless raisins

salt
butter for greasing
¼ pint (⅔ cup) milk
2 oz (4 tablespoons) butter
1 tablespoon (1¼) fine sugar
1 teaspoon (1¼) ground cinnamon
2 oz (½ cup) plain flour

First break the noodles into very small pieces. Cook and drain them in boiling salted water as described on page 23 but using half the quantity of salt.

Rub the cheese through a sieve. Whisk the egg yolks until smooth and beat these into the cheese. Add the cream, sugar, raisins and a pinch of salt. Rub a baking dish with butter. Combine the noodles with the cheese mixture, stir well but gently. Turn the whole into the dish. Add half the milk.

Beat the measured quantity of butter with the fine sugar until creamy. Add the cinnamon and nuts, then gradually add the flour – enough to make the mixture crumbly – a little more or less may be required, it depends on the flour. Sprinkle over the top of the noodles and add the remaining milk. Bake in a moderately hot oven (375°F., mark 5) for 30–45 minutes or until the top is a golden brown. Serve hot.

Instead of breaking wide noodles into short pieces, I prefer to use ricciutelle or farfalle, both of which are light delicate pasta shapes and marry well with the remaining ingredients in this recipe, which is from Central Europe but of ancient Italian origin.

SWEET MACARONI PUDDING

$\frac{1}{4}$ lb macaroni

2 pints (2$\frac{1}{2}$) milk

1 small piece vanilla pod

4 oz (1 cup) sugar

3–4 eggs, well beaten

$\frac{1}{4}$–$\frac{1}{2}$ cup ($\frac{1}{3}$–$\frac{2}{3}$) brandy or rum

1 cup (1$\frac{1}{4}$) thick cream

Put the macaroni into a heavy saucepan with the milk and vanilla pod and bring quickly to the boil. Lower the heat and cook gently until the macaroni is tender. The cooking time will depend on the kind of macaroni used but it will take longer than if cooked in the usual manner, i.e. in boiling water. Stir from time to time, and add the sugar about 20 minutes after the macaroni has been cooking.

Take the pan from the stove. Remove the vanilla pod. Add the eggs, a little at a time, they must be gently but firmly stirred into the pudding. Return the pan to the stove and, stirring all the time, bring to a gentle boil, the eggs must thicken to a sauce. Add the brandy and finally the cream, still stirring. This time let the macaroni cook only until the cream is heated. Do not on any account let it come to the boil. Take the pan from the heat and gently stir the macaroni until it is cool enough to pour into a glass serving dish. Serve cold, preferably topped with coarsely-pounded macaroons.

MACARONI AND CREAM CHEESE PUDDING

$\frac{1}{4}$ lb short macaroni shapes

$\frac{3}{4}$ lb (1$\frac{1}{2}$ cups) cream cheese

butter for greasing

4 egg yolks

2 oz ($\frac{1}{3}$ cup) ground almonds

2 tablespoons (2$\frac{1}{2}$) seedless raisins

2–3 tablespoons sugar

vanilla flavouring

grated rind 1 lemon

Cook the macaroni in boiling lightly salted water as described on page 23. While it is cooking, rub the cheese through a sieve. Rub a round casserole with butter. Beat the egg yolks, add to the cheese, then add the remaining ingredients. Drain the macaroni, spread a layer at the bottom of the casserole, add a layer of creamed cheese. Repeat these layers until all the ingredients are finished; the top layer should be of macaroni. Bake covered in a moderate oven (350°F., mark 4) for about 30 minutes. When the pudding is cooked, it can be turned out, rather like a cake.

Use ricciutelle or other short shapes in this recipe.

MACARONI AND RAISIN PUDDING

6 oz (2½ cups) macaroni (chifferi rigati or similar shapes)
2 pints (2½) milk
½ cup (⅔) seedless raisins
butter for greasing

3 eggs
a pinch of salt
3 oz (⅓ cup) sugar
grated nutmeg or cinnamon

Bring the milk just to the boil. Add the macaroni and raisins and cook steadily for 10 minutes. Rub a large round casserole with butter. Transfer the macaroni, milk and raisins to the casserole. Cover and bake in a hot oven (400°F., mark 6) for 15 minutes. Stir gently from the bottom to prevent the macaroni sticking. Bake another 15 minutes. Beat the eggs with the salt and sugar until smooth. Take the pudding from the oven. Take some of the milk and mix with the beaten eggs. Add this mixture to the macaroni. Stir well to distribute the eggs. Sprinkle lightly with nutmeg, cover and bake in a moderate oven (350°F., mark 4) for another 45 minutes or until the pudding is firm. Serve warm or cold with cream.

BAKED ANGEL'S HAIR PUDDING

¼ lb angel's hair (capelli d'angelo)
1 pint (2½ cups) milk
3 tablespoons (3¾) sugar

2 oz (4 tablespoons) butter
2 eggs, separated
fine breadcrumbs

Bring the milk to the boil, add the angel's hair and stir well. Add the sugar and most of the butter (leave enough to rub the baking dish). Stir well and cook over a low heat for 10 minutes.

Beat the egg yolks. Turn the angel's hair into a mixing bowl. Add the egg yolks, a little at a time and stirring all the while to prevent curdling. Leave to cool. Beat the egg whites until stiff but not dry. Fold these into the angel's hair with a metal spoon, mixing well but gently. Grease a baking dish with the remaining butter and sprinkle round the sides and bottom with bread-crumbs (very dry cake crumbs can be used instead). Add the pudding mixture.

Put the dish in a baking pan and add enough hot water to come half-way up the sides of the dish. Bake in a moderate oven (350°F., mark 4) for 30–45 minutes or until the pudding has risen yet is firm to the touch. Serve hot or cold.

ANGEL'S HAIR PUDDING WITH NUTS

¼ lb angel's hair (capelli d'angelo)
1 oz (2 tablespoons) butter
2 pints (5 cups) milk
4 tablespoons (5) sugar
sultanas, pistachio nuts and crushed
white cardamom seeds

Heat the butter in a saucepan and fry the angel's hair until it becomes a golden brown. Stir all the time as it browns quickly. Add the milk, bring rapidly to the boil, then lower the heat but continue to boil for 10 minutes. Add the sugar, stir it well into the angel's hair and continue boiling gently for a further 10–15 minutes. Stir frequently. Add the sultanas and pistachios and, just before serving, sprinkle the top with cardamom seeds. Serve either warm or cold but preferably cold.

ANGEL'S HAIR PUDDING WITH CHOCOLATE

¼ lb angel's hair (capelli d'angelo)
4 oz (4 squares) cooking chocolate
1 pint (1¼) milk
3 tablespoons (3¾) granulated sugar
butter for greasing
5 egg whites
fine bread or cake crumbs
6 oz (¾ cup) fine sugar

Bring the milk to the boil, add the granulated sugar, stir, then add the angel's hair. Cook until soft, about 7 minutes, the mixture should be fairly thick. Rub a baking dish with butter. Melt the chocolate until it is soft but not runny and beat it until smooth. Beat 2 egg whites until stiff and fold this into the chocolate. Mix this into the cooked angel's hair and turn into the buttered baking dish. Sprinkle lightly with crumbs. Beat the remaining 3 egg whites until stiff, add half the fine sugar and continue beating until a thick consistency is reached. Fold in the remaining fine sugar. Spread this over the top of the pudding and bake in a low oven (325°F., mark 3) until the top of the meringue is lightly tipped with colour.

For those who find meringue toppings rather too sweet, I recommend the following:

2 oz (½ cup) shelled coarsely-chopped nuts
3 oz (⅓ cup) brown sugar

vanilla flavouring to taste
1 egg white, stiffly beaten

Combine the above ingredients and spread this over the top of the cake and bake in a slow oven (as above) until the top is brown.

This pudding can be served hot or cold and, when cut, looks and tastes like a chocolate cake. It is of Viennese origin.

LITTLE STARS WITH A WALNUT AND BUTTER SAUCE

½ lb little stars (stellette)
2 oz (1 scant cup) walnuts

4 oz (8 tablespoons) butter
4 oz (1 cup) brown sugar

Finely chop the walnuts but do not grind them. Cook the stellette in plenty of boiling lightly-salted water for 10 minutes. While they are cooking, melt the butter in a frying pan, add the walnuts, cook for 1 minute, add the sugar and continue cooking until the sugar has melted. Put aside but keep warm, otherwise the sugar will harden. Drain the stellette, turn into a warm serving dish, add the sauce, mix lightly and serve.

Note: If serving this dish for a special occasion (and it is worth doing), add about ½ cupful of brandy to the pan with the walnuts, cook it gently over the lowest possible heat for 1 minute to warm the brandy and let its flavour penetrate the sauce, and then ignite. Leave until the flames die down and pour the sauce over the drained stellette.

CHAPTER TEN

CHILDREN'S DISHES

VEGETABLE SOUP

The vegetables used in this recipe will depend on taste and season. They should be carefully cleaned, trimmed, seeded, etc., and coarsely chopped.

3 oz (¾ cup) stars, little eyes, etc.   *salt*
  (pastina)   *½ oz (1 tablespoon) butter*
2 cups (2½) chopped vegetables

Put the vegetables with 3 pints (7 cups) of water with salt into a pan and bring to the boil. Lower the heat and cook for 1–1½ hours. Drain off the vegetables (these can be discarded), bring the liquid once more to the boil and add the pastina, stirring carefully. Cook until tender. Add the butter and stir well. Serve at once.

If children like cheese and are old enough to accept and digest it, a little grated cheese can be added to the soup.

SWEET CINNAMON-FLAVOURED SOUP

3 oz (¾ cup) little eyes (occhiolini)   *ground cinnamon and brown sugar*
2 cups (2½) each milk and water   *to taste*
salt

Combine the milk and water, add a pinch of salt and bring to the boil. Add the occhiolini, stir and cook until tender, about 5 minutes. Add the cinnamon and sugar.

To vary the flavour, instead of cinnamon, use nutmeg, or a little vanilla extract or vanilla sugar, or the grated rind of a lemon.

BUTTERED NOODLES

½ lb noodles (fettuccine)   butter

Cook the noodles in rapidly boiling salted water as described on page 23. Drain and mix with plenty of fresh butter, which should be firm, not melted. Stir into the noodles and serve at once.

NOODLE AND APRICOT PUDDING

½ lb noodles (fettuccine)
½ lb dried apricots
salt
3 eggs
4 tablespoons (5) sugar
1½ pints (scant 4 cups) milk

grated nutmeg
2–3 tablespoons (2½–3¾) seedless raisins
1½ oz (3 tablespoons) butter, melted

Soak the apricots overnight or for several hours, then cook in the water in which they have been soaking until tender. Drain and chop.

While the apricots are cooking, cook the noodles in lightly salted water as described on page 23. Drain.

Beat the eggs with the sugar until smooth. Scald the milk and pour this into the eggs, stirring all the time. Add the nutmeg, apricots, raisins, noodles and the melted butter. Turn into a baking dish and bake in a moderate oven (350°F., mark 4) for 30–45 minutes or until the custard has set. Serve hot.

MACARONI WITH CURD CHEESE AND CINNAMON

1 lb macaroni (any short cut pasta)   *½ pint (1¼ cups) warm milk*
½ lb (1 cup) curd cheese   *sugar to taste*
½ teaspoon (⅔) ground cinnamon

Cook the macaroni in boiling lightly salted water as described on page 23. While it is cooking, combine curd cheese, cinnamon, milk and sugar. Beat until smooth. Drain the macaroni, turn into a hot casserole, add the sweet sauce and serve at once.

This is a favourite dish with Italian children and is, indeed, one of the oldest methods of cooking macaroni in Italy.

NOODLES WITH CREAMED BANANA SAUCE

½ lb noodles (fettuccine)   *1 cup (1¼) milk*
2–3 ripe bananas, mashed   *4 oz (½ cup) sugar*
2 oz (4 tablespoons) butter   *1 egg*
1 oz (2 tablespoons) plain flour   *1 cup (1¼) double cream*

Cook the noodles in boiling lightly salted water as described on page 23.

Melt the butter, add the flour and stir until thick and smooth. Gradually add the milk, stirring continuously to a thick sauce. Add the sugar and continue cooking for 3 minutes.

Beat the egg until smooth in a mixing bowl. Gradually add the hot sauce, stirring continuously to prevent curdling. Return to the pan and cook over a low heat, stirring all the time, for 2–3 minutes. Take from the heat, add the mashed banana and finally the cream. Put aside but keep warm.

Drain the noodles and divide into six bowls. Pour sauce over each portion and serve at once.

Cravattine and ricciutelle also can be used in the same manner.

MACARONI IN MILK

½ lb macaroni (any of the short   4 oz (½ cup) sugar
  shapes)   1 teaspoon (1¼) ground cinnamon
2 pints (5 cups) milk

Cook the macaroni in boiling slightly salted water as described
on page 23, but for 3 minutes less than the package directs.
Drain, return to the saucepan, add the milk, stir and bring to the
boil. Cook over a moderate heat, the milk gently boiling all the
time for 5 minutes. Add the sugar and cinnamon, stir well and
serve at once.

INDEX

al dente, 25
angel's hair pudding, baked, 147
  with chocolate, 148
  with nuts, 148

breadcrumbs, 35
  buttered, 139

Canelloni
  cheese filling for (and large pasta
    shapes), 140
  meat stuffing for, 139
  stuffed with soft cheese, 110
  with a cheese sauce, green and white,
    109
  spinach and cheese-stuffed, 109
cheese, 34
classical method for cooking pasta, 23
conversion of metric measures into
  British measures, 8
cooking time for boiling pasta in
  water, 10
  in stock, 12

fats, cooking, 34

gnocchi with cream and Parmesan
  cheese, 98

herbs, 35

Lasagne
  baked (1), 106; (2), 107
  Bologna fashion, baked, 107
  and cream cheese, 108
  how to cook, 24
  with prawns or shrimps, 52
Little bows
  with frankfurter sausages, 88
  with a paprika sauce, 88
Little quills with a cheese sauce, 89

Macaroni
  with anchovy and garlic sauce, 50
  with aubergine and tomato sauce, 93
  and bacon casserole, 111
  with bacon and tomatoes, 61
  with creamed banana sauce, 153
  with black olives and salami, 54
  with Bolognese sauce, baked, 98
  with a brandy sauce, 59
  with broccoli, 87
  with brown beans, 58
  with butter and sage, 62
  with capers, anchovies and black
    olives, 54
  and cauliflower cheese, 111
  cheese, 122
  with melted cheese, 112
  with cream cheese, 57
  and cheese custard, 92
  with curd cheese and cinnamon, 153
  and chicken pie, 115
  scalloped chicken and, 114
  with courgettes, baked, 113
  with fish, baked, 51
  with Gorgonzola cheese, 57
  au gratin, 97, 99, 120
  with ham, baked, 112
  with ham and cheese, 100
  and hard-boiled eggs, casserole of, 99
  and meat casserole, 116
  and meat custard, 92
  with ground meat, 95
  with a rich meat sauce, 55
  in milk, 154
  with a mushroom sauce, baked, 120
  and canned mushroom sauce, 60
  with mushrooms and tomatoes, 93
  with mussels, 52
  omelette – Italian style, 121
  with onions, 116
  with onion sauce, 100
  with onion and tomato sauce, 95

Macaroni—*cont.*
with paprika sauce, 56
with peas, 60
with peas, baked, 100
with a pine nut sauce, 87
with pork, 118
in prawn (shrimp) sauce, 49
pudding, sweet, 146
and cream cheese, 146
and raisin pudding, 147
ring, 114
and canned salmon custard, baked,
50
in scallop shells, 94
shepherdess style, stuffed, 96
soufflé, 105
stuffed, 91
with tomato and egg sauce, 62
in 'velvet sauce', 61
with a walnut sauce, 56
with a white wine sauce, 58
mushrooms, 35

Noodles
with almonds, baked, 142
and apricot pudding, 152
with artichokes, 70
with creamed banana sauce, 153
with brandy raisin sauce, 67
with butter and Parmesan cheese, 71
buttered, 152
with white cabbage, 69
cheese soufflé, 104
with chicken, 66
with chicken liver sauce, 70
with courgette sauce, 63
with cream cheese (1), 68; (2), 68
with cream cheese (pudding), 144
with curd cheese and walnuts, 145
custard, baked, 141
with fennel, 69
with garlic, parsley and oil sauce, 67
fried, 118
with honey, 142
with meat and vegetables, 66
omelette, 121
with a parsley and walnut sauce, 63
and pâté, 71
with pesto, 65
with a piquant sauce, 71
with poppy seeds, 144
pudding, baked, 141
pudding, layered, 143
ring, 102
with sauerkraut, fried, 122

'straw and hay' with a chicken
liver sauce, 64
with a cream sauce, 64
with a tomato sauce, 65
and vegetables, casserole of, 101
with walnuts, 143

oils, cooking, 33
olive oil, 33
oven temperature chart, 9

Pasta
buying, 31
draining of, 26
how to cook, classical method, 23
how to cook, new method, 24
how to eat, 27
some guidelines for, 32
how to recognize good, 32
how to serve, 27
oven cooking for, 27
pointers, 30–1
quantity of, 27
shapes, 28–9
storing, 31
without eggs, 30
water for, 26

Quills with a dried mushroom sauce, 89

Salad
dressing, 138
gnocchi and vegetable, 126
macaroni, 125
macaroni and fish, 124
macaroni with veal or chicken, 126
macaroni and vegetable, 125
spaghetti, 126
spaghetti and sweet pepper, 127
stuffed sweet peppers, 124
Sauce
anchovy, 133
anchovy with garlic and hard-
boiled eggs, 134
anchovy and tomato, 133
bacon, 132
Béchamel, 138
Bolognese, 129
butter, cream and cheese, 135
chicken liver, 132
ham and mushroom, 132
herb, 137
lobster, 135
meat, 130
meat, for lasagne, 131

Sauce—*cont.*
  mushroom, 136
  oil, garlic and chilli, 139
  pesto, 137
  sausage meat, 131
  tomato (plain), 128
  tomato (rich), 128
  cream of tomato, 129
  uncooked tomato, 129
  tunny fish, 134
  tunny fish and mushroom, 134
  walnut, 136
  thick white, 138
soufflé, Empress, 104
soufflé recipes, tip for, 103
Soup
  angel's hair, 41
  angel's hair with eggs and cheese, 41
  bean, with chifferini rigati, 40
  Belle Hélène, 38
  cauliflower, with avemaria, 38
  chicken and onion, with puntette, 38
  sweet cinnamon-flavoured, 151
  courgette, with stellette, 39
  egg and cheese, with pisellini, 37
  green pea, with ditalini, 39
  macaroni, 41
  onion and potato, with chinesini, 40
  Swiss, 37
  tortellini in consommé or clear
    stock, 42
  vegetable, 151
Spaghetti
  with anchovies and buttered bread-
    crumbs, 86
  with anchovy sauce, 44
  with anchovy and tunny fish sauce,
    44
  with a bacon sauce, 76
  with bacon and egg sauce, 77
  with bacon, ham and croûtons, 77
  with Béchamel sauce, 83
  Bologna style, 78

  with butter and Parmesan cheese, 82
  with capers and black olives, 81
  with a Champagne and butter sauce,
    80
  with cheese and pepper, 73
  with cream cheese (1) and (2), 73
  with clams, 45
  with crab meat, baked, 46
  Creole style, 123
  devilled, 102
  with egg and cream sauce, 85
  with eggs and sausage meat, 79
  fritters 119
  with garlic and oil, 83
  with garlic and pepper sauce, 83
  with lamb, baked, 103
  with lamb cutlets, 79
  with mussels or clams, 46
  with parsley, 82
  with pork sausage and white wine
    sauce, 80
  with a red wine sauce, 81
  Riviera style, 78
  rustic style, 72
  sailor's style, 45
  with canned salmon, 47
  with sardine and olive sauce, 47
  with shrimp sauce, 48
  with tomatoes and black olives, 76
  with a tomato sauce, 85
  with a tomato and bacon sauce, 74
  with a tomato and meatball sauce, 74
  with an uncooked tomato sauce, 86
  with an uncooked tomato and cheese
    sauce, 75
  with tunny fish, 48
  with white wine sauce, 84
  with yoghourt, 84
spices, 36
spirals with a mushroom sauce, 90
stars with a walnut and butter sauce,
  little, 149

tomatoes, 34